Stories
with Oil
Stains

The World of Women 'Digest' Writers in Pakistan

Kiran Nazir Ahmed

OXFORD
UNIVERSITY PRESS

OXFORD
UNIVERSITY PRESS

Oxford University Press is a department of the University of Oxford.
It furthers the University's objective of excellence in research, scholarship,
and education by publishing worldwide. Oxford is a registered trade mark of
Oxford University Press in the UK and in certain other countries

Published in Pakistan by
Oxford University Press
No. 38, Sector 15, Korangi Industrial Area,
PO Box 8214, Karachi-74900, Pakistan

First Edition published in 2020

ISBN 978-0-19-940898-6

Typeset in Minion Pro
Printed on 68gsm Offset Paper

Mas Printers, Karachi

Acknowledgements
Cover image: © Sweet Art/Shutterstock

Stories with Oil Stains

The World of Women 'Digest' Writers in Pakistan

To attachments (of emotion, intellect, kinship, desire, and memory)

Contents

Acknowledgements

I have accumulated huge debts of gratitude towards a host of people over the course of this research. My first debt is to the writers, editors, and readers of the Urdu genre of popular fiction, published in a form of a magazine known as a 'digest', who shared their world and showed me the importance of listening to 'what the heart experiences'. Your names remain concealed, but your presence permeates this book. It scarcely needs to be said that it is your time and shared moments that made this work possible.

I began the research under the guidance of my dissertation advisor, Kamran Asdar Ali, who is a model of how intellectual rigour can combine with emotional warmth; he continued to patiently read drafts of this work and provide feedback (invariably with humour and warmth) when he was already much burdened. It is a testament to his intellectual generosity that he continued to engage with this work, pushing me to refine my argument even after his official responsibility as dissertation advisor was over and these pages were on their way to their current book form. I hope that I am able to extend the same generosity and unconditional support that he does to his students.

To my committee members at the University of Texas (UT) at Austin. Pauline Strong, who provided thorough and wise advice, and imparted valuable lessons about paying attention and ethical responsibility. Kathleen Stewart revealed new ways of thinking and listening, the importance of slowing down to direct our thought in new ways, and how to dwell in uncertainty. Her greatest gift, however, was to impart confidence and faith in one's work when one most needs it. Barbara Harlow decided to take on my project notwithstanding my lack of training in literary theory and provided insightful advice and linkages which I was unable to initially visualise. She passed away on 28 January 2017, making this world a lesser place. I share her loss with hundreds, if not thousands, of other students and friends who were fortunate enough to benefit from her guidance. Her careful reading and thought-provoking comments in the form of a two-page letter is now a treasured memento.

Over the past few years, I also lost two other dear teachers: David Goicoechea and Imran Hameed. They are both gone but not forgotten because their lectures and conversations remain and continue to shape their students' worldview.

My teachers at Brock University—Ric Brown, George Nathan, Raj Singh, and Johanna Tito—I am grateful to each of you for introducing me to philosophy and what it can offer.

Friends in Austin and in Pakistan: if I were to recount your names or relate what each of you mean to me, these acknowledgements would be longer than the book itself. Suffice it to say, our shared stories, inside jokes, and affinity are very dear to me. Thank you to each of you for your presence, warmth, and friendship.

The camaraderie and togetherness of students and colleagues at the Centre of Excellence in Gender Studies, Quaid-i-Azam University (QAU), continues to be invaluable. Thanks also to my colleagues and seniors at QAU for facilitating an environment where I could hone the work to its present form. Once my manuscript was complete, two anonymous reviewers helped me to further refine it, and I would also like to thank them for their reading.

I am also grateful to the American Institute of Pakistan Studies and South Asia Institute for their financial and institutional support.

Finally, I cannot adequately muster the words to express the love and appreciation my family continues to shower upon me: my father, Nazir Ahmad, and my mother Zahida Kausar; brothers:

Lala, Pasha bhai, Tauheed bhai, Tishi bhai; and sisters: Neely, Zaza, and Aapa; their spouses; my nieces and nephews; and the extended family of cousins. The strength I draw from having you all in my life is immeasurable. Last, and most lovingly, my dear sons, Zan and Ibraheem; you're my pride and joy.

Kiran Nazir Ahmed
November 2017
Islamabad

Introduction

Let us begin with the image of a handwritten story. The writer of this story, a young girl we will call Raheela, initially wrote it for herself in order to improve her Urdu handwriting without the repetitiveness workbooks entail. Gradually, the two characters took acquired form, and she sent it for publication as digest fiction. The story was well received; however, Raheela did not share the news of its publication with many people. This is because there is a dilemma in choosing to publish something in a women's digest. Digest fiction is the highest circulated genre of its kind in Pakistan and therefore reaches the widest possible readership of any form of magazine. However, being identified as a digest writer entails connotations of not being a 'real' writer.

I find myself thinking of Raheela and her stories as I attend a literary festival in my home town, Islamabad. These festivals began in 2010 and are now annually held in three major urban cities: Islamabad, Lahore, and Karachi. Each festival is free, open to the public, and usually lasts for three days, with three or four concurrent sessions. There is a certain liveliness, a buzz, as crowds move in and out of sessions; people greet each other and glance at books displayed in stalls set up outside the venue. Digests are not displayed in any of these stalls, nor are women digest writers present. I ask an organiser about this, and she explains that they plan to invite them to the next gathering. Most people who attend these literary festivals come from an English-speaking background and are usually unacquainted with women's digests in Urdu. There now is, however, a familiarity with their discourse because of the immensely popular television plays written by women digest writers. As with the print form, these televised plays are extremely popular and resonate with a large population. Therefore, even though digest writers are not considered 'real' writers, their stories circulate widely and shape desires. Let me explain this by introducing my friend Roxy (fictitious name) and her continuing engagement with television plays written by digest writers.

Roxy became a friend when I was wandering around Bari Imam, an area on the outskirts of the capital, Islamabad. I had gone to look for Bijlee, a transgender individual I had met for an interview. She was not home, but her neighbour told me I could meet Roxy instead. We walked across to the hand pump, the sole source of water supply. A few people gathered around the pump; their leisurely strides and quick questions indicated familiarity with one another.

'Zainab, is Shaani home? Have you seen Kiran today?' A medium-built figure in her forties with short hair and crumpled pink clothes opened the door. Roxy welcomed me (into her home as well as her life) with her quiet demeanour. More often than not, our conversations revolved around popular television plays written by digest writers. The area where I lived was privileged; hers was not. However, the proximity to parliament and other state buildings led to fewer power breakdowns. Thus, although procuring a meal was often uncertain in her daily life, electricity was quite regular. She, therefore, frequently filled me in on television dramas I had missed because of load-shedding (scheduled power breakdowns).

R: I watched this one yesterday. It was good, but then you have these other useless [*fazool fazool*] plays; they show love stories and all—it is all lies [*jhoot*].

K: But you were also in love.

R: It's all lies [laughing]; it is only for a short time.

Laughing again, she began to tell me about Nadeem, her current boyfriend. Roxy is from a third gender category commonly called Khawaja Siras. Her previous boyfriend struggled with the social pressures of being involved with a Khawaja Sira, and Roxy decided to end the relationship.

R: I said, 'let it be; you be happy with your life, and I'll be happy with mine'.

K: When did you meet your new boyfriend?

R: A few days ago. He works in Aabpara [a local market]. I told him to come to my house at ten, and exactly at ten, he was standing outside my door.

A few days later, as we walked back towards the main road, I asked her what we should do before I left once more for the US. She fancied a movie that was being screened at a nearby cinema hall, so we decided to watch that. Roxy added excitedly, 'Yes, and we'll take Nadeem along too'. Given Nadeem's discomfort with me, I doubted whether he would be willing to join in, but the idea of Nadeem joining us for an outing appeared to resonate with Roxy.

Her favourite scenes from the recent Urdu television play based on the story we began with were those where the hero is taking the heroine out to dates. She termed it 'ghummana phiraana', a term that has connotations of one person taking responsibility for another's sightseeing or entertainment. The play itself revolves around a young girl from an underprivileged background who, through education, succeeds in securing her own and her family's financial circumstances. The privileged boy, who had always caused difficulties for her as a classmate, eventually falls in love with her and marries her. The scenes Roxy enjoyed most are from the last few episodes where he is taking her out for dinners and outings after their wedding. Thus, although a part of her saw the plays as 'jhoot' (lies or deception), another engaged with particular depictions of romance. In Roxy's life, particularly her relationship with Nadeem, several categories of these thematic tables are overturned. Like the woman in the play, Roxy too struggles financially, but education is simply not an option for her. Instead, she frequently has to engage in sex work, performances, or beg to make ends meet. Unlike the hero of the play, who insisted on putting money into his wife's wallet notwithstanding her hefty monthly income, Nadeem is unable to support Roxy, much less take her for outings as the play depicts. Marriage is simply not an option: Nadeem already has a wife, and Roxy, as a Khawaja Sira, has a slim prospect of marrying him. Even so, in the face of all the contradictions, digest discourse had reached Roxy and shaped some of the desires she nurtured for her relationship with Nadeem.

This book follows such ironies and contradictions between 'imaginary worlds' and 'real lives' experienced by Raheela and others whose stories resonate with many in the form of popular fiction and yet are disavowed as having no literary merit. In following such stories, this work presents an ethnography of women writers' engagements with fiction and with each other as writers for the digest form of literature. Digest fiction is a genre published in commercial Urdu monthly magazines called digests.[1] These are primarily stories of domesticity written by and for women in Pakistan.[2] There is of course the possibility of men writing under a pseudonym. However, the very act of assuming a feminine pseudonym points to the perception of these digests as women's space.[3]

These stories are extremely popular and have the highest circulation among all fiction genres sold in Pakistan. Figures for 2015 show a range of circulation for various digests varying from 100,000 to 250,000.[4] However, circulation figures do not accurately portray the actual readership of these digests, as one digest is shared among a number of readers (neighbours, family members). In addition, they are also often resold to used-book shops, where another reader purchases them at half price and then shares them with her family and acquaintances. In other words, although 250,000 copies of a magazine are actually sold, the circle of readers it reaches far exceeds that.

Notwithstanding (or perhaps because of) its popularity, this genre is usually perceived socially as frivolous and pandering to a demand for easy reading.[5] Like most other romance genres, these narratives are often very problematic. The problems range from espousing conventional norms of beauty to stereotypical depictions of gender roles. Feminist work on these digests has highlighted these problems. The first major work was by the National Institute of Psychology in 1984, led by the psychologist Seema Pervez. This was followed by a 1997 study by Uks, a non-profit organisation which works with women and the media. Both studies conducted a textual analysis and came to similar conclusions. The psychologist Seema Pervez concludes that the most popular central idea in digest narratives was that marriage and romance are the most important aspects of a woman's life. She highlights that 'the female protagonist behaves in an emotional way and failure in love destroys her whole life' (1984: 50–1). Similarly, the feminist scholar Tasneem Ahmar (1997) points out:

> Much of the material in these magazines is written in an intensely emotional idiom. The style may well appeal to readers thirsty for pulp entertainment but it also drives home a quintessentially conservative message. Whether deliberately or unintentionally, this literature strips women of their individual identity. They are shown to exist solely through their relationship with men, whether as wife, daughter, cook, or mother.[6]

These are important findings to consider. I am not disputing that these narratives are not problematic or patriarchal. However, there is a need to go beyond a quick funnelling into good/bad, retrogressive/progressive, and to examine other dynamics that are also present here. Moreover, as Edward Said (1983) aptly suggests, although textual analysis (through frameworks such as psychodynamic analysis of a story) yields valuable insights, it also leads to a certain form of rootlessness, as it positions texts in a vacuum. This is because it does not take into account the larger dynamics of power and discourse which permeate the world which the authors inhabit. This is relevant for our purpose here because the problems in these narratives reflect the cultural, social, and political dynamics in contemporary Pakistan. Stereotypes about social life suffuse these stories too, but so do other lived realities, desires, and imagined possibilities.

Digest writers come from a diversity of geographical, educational, and ethnic backgrounds, so there are different vantage points that their stories illuminate.[7] Given the position of these digests as catering to a demand for reading romantic stories, becoming a writer for this genre is not socially prestigious, respectable, or financially lucrative. Therefore, although socially constituted norms are often woven into these fictional accounts, the very decision to write is taken independently in the face of social and familial pressure. Janice Radway (1984) highlights a similar phenomenon when she observes that romantic fiction read by women is based on socially constituted norms, but the very act of reading requires carving out time from familial obligations. As I explain in 'Chapter 2', part of the motivation for writing often comes from the role these digests play as a forum where different vantage points of the lived reality (or imagined possibilities) of being a woman in Pakistan are shared. These depictions of experiences, conflicts, and/or desires resonate with large strata of the population which explains the high circulation figures.

Moreover, this is a space where women do not just articulate their engagement with contemporary moments in Pakistan but also engage with each other on the basis of these articulations. Given the proliferation of mobile phones in recent years, writers frequently communicate with one another (and their readers) in this way. This entails physical absence and anonymity. Readers and writers rarely meet one another, so visual cues of ethnicity, class, and age are absent here. Besides, the editors' caution about politics (being seen as aligning with one political party or another) has created a culture where readers and writers usually keep their political or ethnic affiliations in the background. Therefore, although this genre is often problematic in its depictions of gender, as suggested by Pervez and Ahmer, it has also led to a community where women engage with one another in new ways. In usual contexts, our identities (ethnicity, political leanings, age, class) and roles (such as mother, worker, student, teacher) shape our conversations and what we share with another. In this community, conversations shape identities—an individual becomes known through what they share (about their emotions or relationships) in conversations with other writers or readers. Thus, as I elaborate in 'Chapter 2', usual markers such as age, class, ethnicity, and political affiliations are superseded by the inner world of emotions.

Let me elaborate what I mean by politics receding into the background. At one level, of course, politics permeates everything, so the writers' selection of lived moments for literary depiction, framing of characters, and the editorial act of active omission, are all political choices and drawn from a particular worldview. However, there are certain aspects or topics that are perceived as being explicitly political, in the narrow sense of the word (such as direct critique of the government or a political party), and are therefore censored or changed. For instance, a story about floods and the havoc they wreaked was published but the last section, which directly named a political party as responsible for the damage, was censored. Similarly, patriotism in the form of returning to one's homeland or remaining there notwithstanding other options is often depicted but open criticism of a government, whether military or democratic, is absent. These omissions often arise from editorial concerns about being seen as aligning with one government or political party against another, and related fears of the publisher being attacked or threatened.[8]

In this context, ethnic or political affiliations are silenced. Thus, the usual identity markers in the Pakistani context, such as regional attachments or political ideologies, remain in the background, giving way to a sociality that is based on a mutuality of feelings and experiential knowledge of what it is like to live as a woman. In other words, an individual's identity as a reader or writer is predicated on her views about relationships, morality, and what it means to be a Pakistani woman rather than on ethnic or political loyalties. In this sense, the digest community becomes a space for women that promises 'a certain experience of belonging and provides a complex of consolation, confirmation, discipline, and discussion on how to live as an X' (Berlant, 2008: vii). In this case, the X being a Pakistani woman. Therefore, the decision to engage with this genre and its readers or writers, is a political choice, but one that is outside the usual parameters of politics based on ethnic or political affiliations.

The anthropologist, Kamran Asdar Ali (2012), highlights a similar dynamic in his work on working-class women in Karachi. He suggests that although the reality of conflict is present, there is also an emergent politics that is defined by engagements of cooperation between women of varying ethnicities. Similarly, anthropologist Laura Ring (2006) identifies a bonding that goes beyond ethnic affiliations. Her work is on the everyday lives of women of different ethnicities and religious sects who share the same space (a middle-class, high-rise building in Karachi). In this context, her key argument is that women's daily creative labour (helping each other, exchanging food items, and managing 'male anger') is not consciously undertaken but forms the fabric that enables families with diverse ethnic and political affiliations to live together. In all three cases, this is a politics that is 'a "somewhere else", an "outside" beyond the modalities of organised attempts to help the vulnerable' (Ali, 2012: 602), as political and religious affiliations remain in the background and allow for new norms of engagement to emerge. In Ali's work, it emerges through the shared experience as women go through phases of anxiety and fear of harassment when navigating public spaces. In Ring's work, it takes the form of daily creative labour in a shared physical space, whereas in the digest community, it takes the form of bonds based on shared feelings that grow out of engagement with the shared belonging as readers of a particular genre of fiction.

Besides, as literary theorist Karen Littau (2006) argues, as rational beings we know that fiction is not reality yet it is a precondition of reading fiction to suspend disbelief because only then can one experience the pleasures of fright, sadness, and other emotions. We experience an 'incoherent I' through fiction reading as our usual solidity as an autonomous subject is dissolved. She suggests that this is not always a simple case of identifying with the characters and feeling what they feel, but that these affective delights can also be visceral in nature (2006: 74–6). In this context, Littau believes that the relationship of reader and text is also a bodily one. This is not just in the sense of our perception of a book's ideas being affected through its material form but also because reading involves a certain bodily engagement, even if we are only moving our eyes. She draws on the history of reading to show how our current notion of reading as a cognitive, disembodied activity is a recent development.

Historically, the use of tablets for text necessitated reading aloud; youwouldneedtoreadaloudorthetextwouldnotmakesense.[9] At that time, reading was positioned as a physiological activity (similar to going for a walk). This understanding of bodily engagement remained in the initial phase when the print form was first introduced. Thus, concerns about the sudden popularity of the novel were not just ideological but also physiological. Uncontrollable weeping and reading addiction (as a physiological habit similar to drinking) are some recurrent, involuntary, physiological reactions to reading that people shared repeatedly (Littau, 2006: 37–46).

In our age, this concern has now shifted to television viewing and online addiction. However, this shift in conventional understanding does not necessarily mean that the relationship between a reader and text is no longer one between two bodies (the body of the book and body of the reader). Given Littau's evidence, reading appears to have induced reactions that are no longer prevalent, but that does not mean that reading now lacks all affective bodily engagement.

The anthropologist Brian Larkin (2008), in his ethnography on Nigeria, demonstrates how cinemas provide a social space for a collective sensory experience. Similarly, these digest stories provide a space for a private experience: an 'incoherent I' and a suspension of disbelief. Besides, they have also created a community of readers and writers among whom stories are exchanged and created through conversations, not in terms of lies or deceptions but through encounters that allow space for new identities and norms of engagement. Conversations between readers and writers entail an attunement to emotions, but there is also a certain element of flow and dynamism that I elaborate upon later in the book.

Within this larger framework, this book presents an ethnographic account of women writers' engagement both with this genre and the community (of readers and writers) formed around it. Exploring these engagements raises the following questions: How do digest writers develop bonds of trust and friendship in the absence of physical proximity and visual cues (because readers and writers rarely meet one another)? How do the dynamics of anonymity and absence function in this context? How do digest writers depict lived realities—both of attachments in the digest community and the larger dynamics of living as a woman in Pakistan's changing social milieu—through their fictional stories? How do they see fiction writing, and what role do they see it playing in their lives? What specific forms do agency and engagement assume in this context? What challenges or opportunities do writers experience when they enter the arena of script writing for television, and how do they respond to the notions of their writing being inauthentic and frivolous? In exploring this range of questions, this ethnography (and its introduction) traces three key themes: attachment, articulation, and agency.

ATTACHMENT

The French philosopher Jacques Derrida (1967) highlights that although language—and our usual patterns of thought—privilege presence over absence and identity over anonymity, these are false dichotomies; presence involves absence, and absence can often lead to new forms of presence. I draw on this argument to highlight how attachments between readers and writers are textured with anonymity and physical absence that leads to an emergence (or presence) of attachments through new norms of engagement. As I elaborate in 'Chapter 1', the dynamics of anonymity and physical absence arise because readers and writers rarely meet one another; their interaction is in the main through mobile phones. In this context, their identities are largely based on their fictional stories and how they choose to portray their personal lives in conversations.

Given digest editors' wariness of politics, in the narrow sense of the word, political affiliation, ethnic loyalties, and other markers of identity that usually function in everyday life remain in the background, and individual feelings and the inner world become central. In other words, aspects of identity that are usually open and visible, such as ethnic or political affiliations, are not disclosed but private emotions are generously shared. This may be akin to self-censorship, but as anthropologists Kaur and Mazzarella (2009) suggest, although censorship is usually positioned as restrictive, it also has a certain productive aspect. This is because it can also lead to a proliferation of discourse that might not have otherwise emerged. Similarly, editorial censorship or the personal desire to not dwell on political issues leads to the unexpected dynamic of engagements between readers and writers where political and ethnic affiliations are superseded by personal feelings and emotions.

Let me briefly discuss the concept of this personal world which I am privileging here. The literary theorist Janice Radway (1984) argues that fiction entails a suspension of disbelief (enabling us, for example, to experience fear and joy). Moreover, unlike television, reading is a solitary activity. Thus, an individual engages with the emotions being felt by fictional characters in private. This is relevant for our purpose because digest reading facilitates a certain sensibility of connecting with another woman's inner world (shared through fictional stories which depict lived realities or imagined possibilities). This sensibility also carries over to conversations between readers and writers as emotional resonance with desires or depicted experiences lead women to approach a certain writer, and engagement continues to be through emotions and imagined desires (an individual's inner world) rather than the usual markers of identity (nationality, ethnicity, political ideology).

The literary theorist Lauren Berlant (2008) identifies this emotional resonance between women as shared experiential knowledge of 'each other's experience of power, intimacy, desire, and discontent, with all that entails' (Berlant, 2008: 5).[10] She draws on affect theory and suggests that abstract notions such as 'nation' or 'public' attain legitimacy through the affective engagement people have with these identities.[11] In this context, she particularly focuses on the public sphere that both surrounds and grows from media geared towards women, such as these digests. In other words, marginalised groups such as women form an intimate public that has its own processes of identification and engagement. This public is not intimate on the basis of autobiographical sharing as such but because 'consumers of its particular stuff already share a worldview and emotional knowledge that they have derived from a broadly common historical experience' (Berlant, 2008: vii).

While Berlant focuses on attachments as affective engagement, the literary theorist Sharon Marcus (2007) highlights the intensity of emotional engagements between women (through her work on women's life-writings in the Victorian era). Marcus suggests that these friendships were intertwined in ways that go beyond the binary of homosexuality and heterosexuality. I draw on her argument, as there are some striking parallels in what she describes and the contours of the digest community: friendships are formed in absence and exist in tandem with, rather than in opposition to, heterosexual desire. In the chapters that follow, I demonstrate the emotional intensity of women's attachments both through their own depictions (in fictional stories about friendships) and ethnographic account of encounters in the digest community.

The dynamic of anonymity which I earlier suggested (through the use of mobile phones) lends these conversations a certain element of flow and pre-subjectivity that can be explored through the French philosopher Gilles Deleuze's concept of connections and existence as an unfolding of actualisations. As I elaborate in 'Chapter 1', he suggests that actualisations and connections are made not just through human existence, but can also be through relationships, eras, or even body parts. I trace these conversations as Deleuzian connections and further highlight that even though these phone conversations take place through disembodied voices, there is also a certain visceral engagement, as suggested earlier, that arises because of the sensibility of being fiction readers and writers.

ARTICULATION

As shared earlier, scholarship on digest fiction (Ahmer, 1997; Pervez, 1984) highlights how dominant norms of gender, conventional notions of beauty, and women's traditional roles (such as wife or mother) are espoused in these narratives. In contrast, the anthropologist Kamran Asdar Ali (2004) suggests that 'pulp fiction' of the kind represented by digest fiction needs to be interpreted beyond the political framework of the retrogressive–progressive dichotomy by positioning these fictional accounts as specifically 'embedded' in social practices at particular moments in Pakistan. He highlights how these fictional articulations also provide us with a window into the lived realities and imagined desires of contemporary Pakistani women. I draw on his argument and propose that women's stories are their articulation of lived realities as well as imagined possibilities of being a woman in Pakistan.

In positing the question of being a woman as open and ongoing, I draw on the feminist scholar Judith Butler (1990), who frames sex (or the binary of bodies into male and female) as culturally constructed and part of the gender system. Similarly, the anthropologist Evelyn Blackwood (2006) focuses on the difference between dominant ideologies of gender and the spaces or gaps for a disruption of these notions. She suggests that gender comprises two overlapping processes: cultural category and subjective experience. Gendered identities are a way for individuals to make sense of who they are, and these identities are embedded within structures that 'claim constancy and immutability' (Blackwood, 2006: 214). Yet within these very structures are gaps and spaces which permit dissent. I suggest that digest fiction is a site where dominant ideologies of what it means to be a Pakistani woman are reinforced, but the same site also leaves gaps for negotiation and reworking.

South Asian women's journals as a key site for this dual move, articulations and their questioning, is not a new phenomenon. South Asian feminists Susie Tharu and K. Lalitha (1993) identify popular journals for women from the nineteenth and early twentieth centuries as a crucial site where key issues were being negotiated. Similarly, Veer Talwar (1989) traces some of the more influential women's magazines and identifies stories that demonstrate how questions regarding education and veiling were renegotiated through these writings.

Digest writers come from varied socio-economic backgrounds and engage with the question of what it means to be a woman from a discursive standpoint. In this context, they can be posited as 'cultural citizens'. This is a term the anthropologist Rudolph Gaudio (2009) uses to highlight that along with citizenship of the state, there is a fluid framework of cultural citizenship. Our identities are embedded in social fields and institutions. Thus, participation in social worlds means navigating on the basis of particular aesthetics, emotions, and beliefs, not just power relations. This is relevant here because writers consciously examine and articulate their negotiation with prevalent cultural norms of femininity. This discursive engagement is through particular aesthetics, ideas, and sentiments about being a woman that are at times confirmed, appropriated, or contested by other digest writers or readers. In this book I demonstrate that different writers depict and articulate the same lived realities differently by sharing an ethnographic account of four writers and their articulations of their lives and engagement with fiction. In this context, I highlight what the anthropologist Abu-Lughod (1999) in her research on Bedouin poetry terms 'veiled sentiments': feelings that do not enter daily discourse but can be safely articulated through creative expression.

Agency

The anthropologist Saba Mahmood (2001) aptly observes that the notion of agency as striving for personal or collective interests against structural obstacles is not universal. Different cultural or historical vantage points can position agency differently. Drawing on her argument, I trace the specific forms agency takes in the lives of four writers. As I elaborate in 'Chapter 3', at one level, they have displayed both agency and resilience by learning to read and write in the face of overwhelming odds. In this sense, they are evocative of the historian Gail Minault's 'secluded scholars' (1998)—writers in the eighteenth and nineteenth centuries who learned to read and write notwithstanding the odds. However, the larger institutional structures of restricted mobility and lack of education remain the same. In *The History of Sexuality* (1992), Foucault delineates the final forms power takes, such as sovereignty of the state, law, and overall domination, and its strategies as the 'multiplicity of force relations' (1980: 92). In this context, he suggests that 'power is accompanied with resistance', so one is always 'inside power[;] there is no escaping it' (Foucault, 1980: 95). Abu-Lughod builds on this Foucauldian notion of power and its links with resistance. She argues that romanticising resistance as a sign of the ineffectiveness of power structures leads to an overturning of oppositional power structures as the sole criterion for success.

Thus, a better approach to the relationship between power and agency is one of entanglement rather than overturning. Drawing on these frameworks, I present the specific forms agency takes in four writers' lives and then highlight disengagement as a form of agency, as one of the writers has disengaged from fiction because of her dreams.

ETHNOGRAPHIC POSITIONING

My engagement with the writers of this genre began in the early 1980s as a reader. However, my intellectual engagement with this genre and its writers began in 2003 when I began noticing voices of dissent in these commercial magazines. My first academic writing on this subject was a response. As stated earlier, most if not all scholarly work in Pakistan appeared to characterise women's digests as frivolous fiction which frequently eroded notions of much-needed women's agency. Thus, in responding, the effort was to bring forth voices of dissent in this genre which raised important questions in relation to issues such as domestic violence and financial independence.

Anthropological training led to a problematisation of the productive–restrictive binary and a subsequent positioning of digest writers' fiction as a creative site of women's articulations. Ethnographic work for this book began in the summer of 2012 and was conducted over a period of twenty months (summer of 2012 and 2013), followed by a subsequent sixteen months of fieldwork (Sept 2014–Dec 2015). Fieldwork took the form of archival research, participant observation, and semi-structured interviews.

In 2012, I began with a group of twelve writers and two editors (of monthlies entitled *Pakeeza* and *Khawateen Digest*).[12] The writers reside in different parts of Pakistan, so half of these initial interviews were conducted over the phone and half in person. I, however, began realising that the interviews over the phone led to a deeper engagement than those conducted in person. Writers were more forthcoming in terms of sharing their experiences and related to my identity as a reader (rather than an academic). Those I met in person were also very warm and welcoming; however, in those interactions, their role as homemaker appeared to dominate our encounters. Family members trailed in and out of the room, and they were preoccupied with their role as host (for instance, checking whether I had finished my tea and wanted some more). I therefore began to focus on phone conversations and the dynamic of physical absence. Interviews were not conducted in one or two sessions but entailed repeated engagement (ranging from daily to weekly conversations) over a period of twenty months. The level of engagement with each writer varied depending upon her domestic responsibilities and availability. Most of these conversations took place late at night, and some extended to a session of over seven hours. The writers were aware that the conversation was in the context of my book; however, I was primarily positioned as a reader. Therefore, friendship and the shared bond of familiarity with digest discourse textured our relationship.

At one level, I was researching this community but (as I explain in chapters 1 and 4), I was also being examined. Thus, conversations were as much about their questions (about how I felt about certain aspects of life) as they were about my questions about their role as writers. In addition, I also conducted semi-structured interviews with editors (who select and tailor narratives by writers and often become their mentors), admins (volunteers who manage readers' groups through social media), readers, and voluntary non-readers (individuals who are familiar with this genre but choose not to read it). Until the past decade, digest fiction was only available in print form. However, recent developments, such as licensing of private TV channels, their need to fill airtime, and the initial success of televised plays based on digest narratives have created an expanding niche for digest writers in the Pakistani electronic media space.[13]

Quite a number of digest writers are therefore now also working as television script writers. This has meant an exponential increase in financial remuneration. Currently, writers are usually paid about $10 (Rs. 1,000) for a short story and $300 (Rs. 30,000) for a novel. In comparison, the payment for television script writing for established digest writers can be up to $1,000 (Rs. 100,000) for each episode (a television play usually has fifteen episodes). However, as I elaborate in 'Chapter 4', this also entails several problems. To better understand how digest writers were perceived in the electronic media, I held interviews with television channel heads (who televise plays written by digest writers); content managers (who tailor a digest writer's work for television audiences), and script writers (who have an intertextual engagement with digest fiction). In addition, I conducted ethnographic work with new and unexpected audiences, such as members of the transgender community who regularly engage with plays by digest writers (including my friend Roxy, introduced earlier).

Gradually, I became close to certain writers and went on to stay in their homes. In this context, I focused on varying ethnicities and urban versus rural backgrounds. Specifically, I visited the rural areas of two provinces (Sindh and Punjab) and the cities of Islamabad, Rawalpindi, Lahore, and Karachi. This extended to visiting or staying in writers' homes as well as visits to digest offices, television channel offices, and locations where television plays were being shot.

In addition to explicit issues of methodology, there are also implicit aspects that need to be elaborated. I was an insider in the sense that I grew up in my research site. As a digest reader, I was also familiar with the discourse and certain norms of engagement. However, as Patricia Zavella (2003) highlights, as 'insider researchers', what we find relevant about our identity, or what we assume the respondents relate to as common ground, might be very different from how the respondents perceive us. As mentioned earlier, I initially positioned myself as an academic, but the writers positioned me as a reader. This became a strength because it allowed our engagement to follow pathways other than those they might otherwise have been. However, this also led to certain complications. Let me explain this by sharing a self-reflective write-up by a photojournalist. He had gone to cover an incident in his local town. A man accidentally killed his grandchild, who slept in a stroller in the driveway, when reversing his car. As the journalist was taking photos of various angles of the scene, he saw this man sitting alone with his head in his hands. The anguish and grief in his demeanour would have made for a perfect photo. The journalist, however, decided against taking one because he realised it was an intrusion into this man's personal tragedy. The photo might be award-worthy but it would have been at the cost of an instrumental public packaging of an acutely private moment.

I share this story here to articulate some of my own concerns and confusion. How much can one share about another life without violating the norms of decency? Respondents hand over their private life experiences, and we attempt to weave them into an academic framework. We design the construction of our work, but it is the respondents who gift us building blocks by sharing life experiences. In this context, formal modes of interview, participant observation, and focus group discussion all work on an explicit understanding of this exchange. What then about the moments when these dynamics become blurred? An interview conducted during the regular hours of the day (9–5 working hours) has a different temper than a conversation that takes place late at night. The most valuable material I gathered during fieldwork was about these shared intimacies and bonds in this community. As I articulate in 'Chapter 1', private feelings are shared easily, but where does one draw the line? Does personal grief, spontaneously shared in a long, late-night conversation, fall within the realms of an interview? Using the previous analogy, these are some of the most beautiful building blocks, but is it ethical to frame and place them at the forefront of the structure or should they remain hidden and private?

The simplest way is, of course, to ask the individuals who have shared them, and I did. This validation again helped calm some of my concerns, but not completely. In some contexts, the relationship takes precedence over personal discomfort. For instance, you might not be comfortable with what your sister asks of you but still feel obliged to agree to it because she is your sibling. The relationship can take precedence over personal judgement or unease. Similarly, given the deep bonds of affection that gradually developed, I often wondered about the source of this consent. Were they agreeing, notwithstanding discomfort, just to help me? What about the deepest moments of personal sharing: was it ethical to even ask to use them for a document that was going to become public?

Eventually, I decided to do what the writers do with such personal sharing. They often weave these emotions into a fictional narrative with personal details changed so only the person who has articulated those sentiments recognises his or her words. Most familial and personally identifiable details remain private. In a sense, this provided an answer to the photographer's dilemma mentioned earlier. Intimate sentiments can be portrayed, but only if the identifiable face remains veiled. Thus, given the kind of personal details being shared here, the names of most writers have been changed and only the editors' names remain unaltered.

Finally, Abu-Lughod (1991, 2006) problematises the 'speaking to and speaking from' that happens when an insider works on her own culture. She highlights that in these contexts there is a 'complex awareness of and investment in reception' (2006: 156). This book is written in English and directed towards an academic community. It aims at translation and, like all ethnographies, asks the reader to feel the flow and depth of the world explored. The digest community, too, is an audience, but given the language and form this takes, they appeared to be less invested in the final form it took. Some writers did express an interest in how I was representing them, but for the most part, they positioned this as my work. In other words, they largely viewed this book as a requirement that would further my academic career but had little to do with the orbits of circulation that they felt emotionally invested in (such as readers, writers, families, production houses). However, as a digest reader myself, in representing them, I am also, perhaps, representing myself.

Chapter Overview

Chapter 1: In Quest of Anonymity: Bonds of Friendship in the Digest Community

The first chapter explores the bonds that emerge when the usual markers of identity such as age, class, ethnicity, and/or political affiliation remain invisible. In this context, this chapter traces the community of writers as one of sound and physical absence, as the bonds of affection between them and their readers are formed in the absence of visual cues. This chapter traces these dynamics in the context of phone conversations at three different levels: community, subgroups, and dyads. These three levels follow the trajectory of my ethnographic fieldwork which entailed discovering the digest community as one of sound and feelings, becoming part of subgroups, and finally being in a dyad with a specific digest writer. I demonstrate the attunement to emotions in these conversations and suggest that there is also an element of dynamism and flow that can be explored through the philosopher Gilles Deleuze's framework of unfolding actualisations and connections.

Chapter 2: In Quest of Stories: Writers, Readers, and Fiction

This chapter explores digest fiction as a site where various vantage points regarding the fluidly lived reality of being a Pakistani middle-class woman are articulated. It shares two digest stories and traces how digest writers depict lived realities: both of attachments in the digest community and the larger dynamics of living as a woman in Pakistan.

Specifically, I begin by sharing a digest story to demonstrate how writers portray the dynamic of physical absence in their bonds with one another. I highlight the theme of absence and emotional intensity depicted in the story and suggest that this emotional intensity is common in the friendships between readers and writers, yet it exists along with, rather than in contrast to, mainstream notions of heterosexual desire. In this context, I draw on literary theorist Sharon Marcus (2007), who discusses forms of intense engagements between women. The second half of the chapter changes scale to demonstrate how these fictional stories articulate imagined possibilities and lived experiences of being a woman in Pakistan. I draw on two specific theoretical frameworks: the literary scholar Judith Butler (1990), who posits the question of being a woman as open and ongoing, and feminist scholars Susie Tharu and K. Lalitha (1993), who identify South Asian women's journals in the nineteenth and early twentieth centuries as a site where questions such as child marriage and women's education were being negotiated by women. Through these frameworks, I proceed to show how personal desires, lived moments in Pakistan's history, and notions of how a woman should behave texture these narratives by tracing the specific form this takes in a writer's work. I then share a digest story that depicts themes such as women's work empowerment and familial conflict. I contextualise the story by connecting it to specific realities of women's paid employment in Pakistan and then share my own engagement with the same story as a digest reader.

Chapter 3: In Quest of Meaning: Four Women and their Stories

This chapter continues the trajectory of previous ones by examining how different writers depict and engage with the same lived realities. It does so by focusing on four digest writers from the same family who live in a shared household. I draw on Edward Said (1983), who asserts the importance of contextualising texts in the worlds through which they emerge. In this context, I highlight the world of these writers and examine how each of them engages with the given world through her own lens.

Specifically, I explore two concepts: agency and engagement. All four writers are remarkable in that familial norms have not allowed them mobility or education yet, as digest writers, they have been able to both attain literacy and a form of mobility by making their private voices public. As one of them shared, 'I could not become a lawyer or a social worker, but sitting at home I could write stories and become a digest writer.' Thus, writing fiction for digests has become an avenue for agency in the absence of spatial mobility and formal education. This chapter explores the notion of agency by demonstrating the variety of forms it has taken in each writer's life. I draw on the anthropologist Saba Mahmood (2001), who asserts that agency understood as the capacity to realise one's own interests against the weight of obstacles is only one standpoint; there can be other culturally specific forms of agency. I demonstrate that even within the same context of prescribed norms and daily lived lives, agency can assume different meanings. Furthermore, I draw on the anthropologist Lila Abu-Lughod (2000), as her reflections on resistance allow us to go beyond the framework of 'resistance' as valid only if it overturns power structures. In the context of engagements with the world, I discuss the fact that although their bodies have restricted mobility, given their position as faith healers and spiritual leaders, these women writers often witness or undergo experiences that defy mainstream bounds of reality. Through an ethnographic account of my stay with them, I explore how my own assumptions about reality and belief were occasionally overturned when I witnessed their experiences.

Chapter 4: In Quest of Respect: Engagement with the Electronic Media

The last chapter continues the story of digest writers by examining how they make sense of their entry into television and the challenges they have to face, in particular with regard to the social perception of not being 'real' writers. The first section begins by focusing on a popular drama serial to demonstrate the parallel dynamics of commercial success and popularity on the one hand and inauthenticity on the other. It explores the social perception of digest writers as pandering to the lowest common denominator. I suggest that these plays do pander to certain commercial or base desires, but these television depictions of digest fiction also act as an avenue for what can best be described as little slivers of reality: personal experiences of middle-class women which the writers rescue from oblivion. In this context, I present two plays: one of a digest writer, partly based on my personal life, and one that depicts the struggles of a digest writer who becomes a television script writer. I briefly compare the latter to a digest story written in the 1970s to highlight some similarities and differences in how digest writers have continued to address the notion of inauthenticity through their work. I present key themes to show that the struggle for authenticity is in not just the public realm but also the private realm of family. Finally, I follow up on these two key strands, familial disapproval and challenges in the television arena, by narrowing the ethnographic gaze to two writers to show the specific forms it takes in their lives.

In conclusion, this ethnography presents two entwined narratives: the fictional stories written by digest writers about their everyday lives and the ethnographic story I tell about them.

Moreover (as I explain in 'Chapter 4'), during the course of fieldwork, my assumption of one-sided ethnographic gaze was overturned. The gaze was not just reciprocated but also led to a fictional play which had a larger audience than this book will ever have. In other words, our encounters led to not one but two creations: an academic book and a fictional electronic play, each with its own story and orbit of circulation.

At one level, that television play and this book are markedly different in terms of content, circulation, and form. One path is of observation and the other of imagination. This book claims to portray 'what is' whereas the television play is presented as fictional 'what could be'. However, as anthropologist Didier Fassin (2014) aptly highlights, this binary is not airtight. This ethnography aims to present 'what is', but it is through a filter of subjective interpretation. What the respondents communicated forms the content of this work, but some narratives were selected while others never made it past the transcription file. There is also the factor of underplaying certain aspects while accentuating others. Therefore, although depiction is presented as fictional in one case and real in another, ultimately, each is a portrayal and thus assembled and created in a certain sense. What each desires of the audience is also similar. Television plays use camera techniques to draw attention to certain aspects. Similarly, ethnographies use vivid descriptions to highlight certain phenomena. Thus, both carry an implicit invitation to 'notice this, look at that' in an attempt to communicate the richness of the worlds being shared. Therefore, like other ethnographies, this one invites you, the reader, to step into its world of digest writers and to feel its flow and depth.

Notes

1. Urdu is the national language of Pakistan.
2. Historically, digests can be traced back to the very first specialised periodicals for women of the subcontinent which emerged through the

reformist movement of educating Muslim women. In the late nineteenth century, Muslim reformers resisted colonial influence by emphasising Muslim culture and Islamic laws 'as opposed to the realm of custom' (deemed to be superstitious, un-Islamic, and irrational). This, in turn, led to an increased interest in educating Muslim women, especially in north Indian middle- and upper middle-class families. Given the low literacy rates, particularly of women, at the inception of this genre (in 1924, only four of every thousand Muslim women could read and write), circulation was low. Till the 1960s there was little change, but gradually this genre gained circulation. According to advertising expenditure data, the number of magazines in Pakistan increased from 214 in 1993 to 406 in 2000. The majority of these were in Urdu and were women's magazines. The same sources estimate 7 per cent of the total population read these digests (Ali, 2004:125–6).

3. It is important to add here that contrary to the social perception of these digests as being frivolous fiction by and for women, men also read them. The writers generally refer to women as their readers, but a few writers whom I interviewed related specific incidents of men or boys reading their work. Anthropologist Lila Abu-Lughod's framework of 'encounters' between 'performative subjects' is useful in contextualising this building on Homi Bhabha's formulation that 'in nations, the people are both pedagogical objects and performative subjects'; she treats the relationship between producers (Egyptian television drama serials) and audience (viewers of those serials) as a series of encounters:

    These encounters are between the television dramas that seek to shape, inform and educate and those who are the intended objects of this molding ... two sorts of performative subjects – a certain elite who among other things, produces national television for imagined audiences, and various subalterns who not only appreciate and enjoy but critically interpret, select and evaluate what the elites produce ... always in the context of their everyday lives. (2005: 11–12)

    The circulation of these narratives amongst men also points to the same phenomena. The writers and editors frame it pedagogically, according to a particular kind of audience of women they have in mind. Even so, there are overflows and unexpected 'encounters' as these stories are critically evaluated and appropriated not just by the intended readership but also by an unintended readership.

4. Figures obtained through interviews with distributors and editors. Digests entitled *Khawateen Digest* and *Shuaa* are the most widely read (250,000 to 150,000). This is followed by *Pakeeza*, which has a circulation of 90,000 to 100,000. Figures on the urban–rural breakdown are not available. However,

based on the letters sent by readers, there appears to be a large proportion of readers in rural areas.

5. The format of these monthly magazines is relatively simple. They start with an editorial note and end with letters by readers. There are also additional sections on beauty, recipes, and psychological and spiritual advice. The bulk of the pages are devoted to fiction in the form of serialised novels and ten to twelve short stories. Most of the stories printed in these digests can be compared to Harlequin romances in terms of the theme. However, in contrast to the Harlequin portrayal of the central protagonists as autonomous individuals with few family ties (Jensen, 1980), these narratives are predominantly framed within the everyday domesticity of women and extended families.

6. Tasneem Ahmar, 'Pulp Fiction', *The Herald*, December 1997.

7. Rather than a monolithic group, writers come from different age groups, educational backgrounds, and geographical areas. The biggest divide is perhaps in terms of rural and urban regions. Life experiences and basic rights such as educational opportunities are markedly different depending on where you live. For instance within the overall national literacy rate of 58 per cent, the city of Islamabad stands at 87 per cent, while the rural district of Kohlu in Balochistan has a rate of 20 per cent.

8. The role of editors is particularly significant, given their directorial capacities as well as their long tenures. Anjum Ansar has acted as *Pakeeza*'s editor for over 20 years, and Amtul Saboor has served as *Khawateen Digest*'s editor for over 30.

9. The words in this line are without any space, since that is the way it was with stone tablets; when you read it silently, it is difficult to make sense but when you read it out loud, you can grasp it more easily

10. Also see Kathleen Stewart (2015), 'On Regionality', *Geographical Review*, 103(2): 275–84.

11. There is no single generalisable theory of affect (Gregg and Seigworth 2010). It can however be seen as a focus on visceral forces, other than conscious knowing, that drive us towards thought, movement, and changing relations. The overall aim of this approach can be seen as an attempt to create experimental spaces that allow 'new ways of thinking about what may be going on' (Stewart, 2011:445). In this context, the literary theorist Lauren Berlant (2008) uses the term 'intimate public' and observes that the print and electronic media and the publics around it can be viewed as an affective space of belonging which provides a complex of confirmation and consolation on how to 'live as an X' (Berlant, 2008: vii; In tracing the contours of this community as an intimate public I draw on Berlant's work).

12. The underlying assumption for both editors was in terms of the influence these digests have on women and their role of acting in the best interest of their readers. This can sometimes also be at the cost of commercial gain. In this context, Saboor gave the example of an advertisement company which wanted them to print an ad for a facial cream. They were willing to pay a substantial amount but as the cream was relatively expensive, the staff took a stand. They decided to withhold the ad till they had tested it themselves. The product did not live up to its promise and the ad was not printed.

13. In her interview with me, the head of the television channel HUM, which employs most of the digest writers, stated that easy availability of digest writers and their focus on the everyday lives of women led them to telecast plays based on digest narratives (Interview with Sultana Siddiqui, Karachi, June 2013).

1

In Quest of Anonymity: Bonds of Friendship in the Digest Community

چل بُلھیا چل اوتھے چلئے جِتھے سارے اَنھے

نہ کوئی ساڈی ذات پِچھانے نہ کوئی سانوں مَنے

Chal Bulliya chal othay chaliye jithay saaray annay
Naa koi saadi zaat pichanay na koi saanoon mannay

So that no one will run before or behind
let us go to a place where all are blind.[1]

Presence and identity are generally privileged over absence and anonymity. This is usually for good reason, as human interaction without identity and physical presence often becomes an avenue for exploitation, as cases of fabricated online identities, exploitation, or verbal abuse and harassment over the Internet demonstrate. However, in certain contexts, such as the digest community, these dynamics can also lead to deep bonds of connection. This chapter explores the bonds that emerge when the usual markers of identity such as age, class, ethnicity, and/or political affiliation remain invisible. The dynamic of anonymity and physical absence arises because readers and writers rarely meet one another. Their interaction is largely over mobile phones. In this context, their identities are based on their fictional stories and how they choose to portray their personal lives in conversations. Given the digest editors' wariness of 'politics', in the narrow sense of the word, such affiliation with political parties, ethnic loyalties, and other markers of identity that are usually present in everyday life remain in the background, whereas an individual's feelings and inner world become central.

Writers are easily approachable (both by the readers and each other) in the digest community. Previously, they would communicate through published letters mediated by the editors. Some readers also sent letters directly to the writers or occasionally called them. However, given the high cost of long-distance calls and lack of privacy, these were very limited. Now, with the proliferation of mobile phones, readers and writers frequently converse with one another. Therefore, although the stories and letters are in print form, the connection between these groups, their daily contact, and exchange of ideas is over the phone. Moreover, rather than a public forum as such, the conversations (with another writer or reader) take place in a dyad. This private sharing in turn creates friendships that are based on a shared sense of each other's feelings. Physical absence and lack of visual cues bring into being new norms of engagement and allow for the emergence of bonds that overturn the public–private dichotomy as private details of everyday life, relationships, and how one feels about them are shared, whereas public details such as one's age, class, ethnicity, and political affiliations often remain private.

The French philosopher Jacques Derrida (1967) observes that the structure of language and the resulting foundations of thought privilege certain notions over others.[2] Therefore, there is an implicit hierarchy when we speak about presence and absence or identity and anonymity. He suggests that the problem is not just one of hierarchy, but that it creates a false binary: one cannot subsist without the other. There is a blurring of these apparently oppositional contexts. To take a simple example, you are and are not the person you were at the age of seven. That identity is present in certain ways and absent in others. His point, therefore, is that absence is not the opposite of presence; there is an interweaving and an entanglement. This observation is relevant for our purpose here as, in the digest community, anonymity appears to bring about new identities, and physical absence allows new forms of presence to emerge. This chapter traces these dynamics in the context of phone conversations. In this context, it explores questions such as how the digest community functions as one of sound. How are connections formed in the absence of visual cues? What are the key gestures that cement these friendships? How do these friendships interact with familial dynamics? How do dyads function, and what is the texture of emotional intimacy that can form in the process?

THE DIGEST COMMUNITY AS ONE OF SOUND

Given that bonds of affection are formed through phone conversations, the digest community functions as a sound sensorium. In other words, these conversations can be seen as a shared emotional experience where the lack of visual cues leads to voices becoming only that: voices which share life stories and experiences. My aim here is not to explore what this change means but what it does in these relationships. Thus, I trace the contours of conversations on the phone and demonstrate how emotional bonds are formed in the absence of visual cues. In the process, I also highlight the experience of having to use the ethnographic ear rather than the ethnographic eye to converse with writers.

Being with my friend Sara (fictitious name) brought a different way of navigating the world. Food was not piled on the plate; it was placed one item separate from the other and positioned in sync with clock numbers ('Rice is at 6 o'clock, chicken at 10 o'clock', I hear my voice saying to her). Sound stood in for sight. Your body did not signal your presence; your voice announced it. Spatiality was also through sound. Stairs were not just steps; sound proclaimed them as going up or down and assigned a specific number. This world was comfortable for Sara, as she shared, 'Someone at work asked me why I didn't want eyesight. I said because it would mean having to relearn everything.'

Ethnographic fieldwork with writers introduced another world of sound with its own rhythms. Here, writers, editors, and readers are the three entwined voices. These identities are clear but not distinct. Readers become writers, writers continue to be readers, and some editors are also fiction writers for their magazines, and while this is frowned upon, it is tolerated. There are also a large number of readers who continue to be readers, and a segment of writers who have entered the world of television dramas.[3]

Calling one of the numbers published in the magazine, I asked for the editor's contact number. Her home number (she worked from home) was given without asking for any details of who I was or why I wanted it. After several abortive attempts, I decided to try her number again at ten in the morning. After two rings, when I asked for Anjum Ansar Sahiba, a voice told me I was speaking to her.

The contours of this sound community began to emerge as she spoke about receiving twenty-five to fifty calls a day.

> I talk to them as much as I can. Even when I'm asleep, I just take the call, tell the reader I'm asleep and they should call later, and just easily go back to sleep. It doesn't disturb me in any way …. Most of the inspiration for my stories comes from the real stories I hear from *Pakeeza* [the digest she edits and writes for] readers who call.

Her serialised novel is also drawn from a story related by a reader. Entitled *Kaanch si larki* (A Girl as Fragile as Glass), the novel portrays the trauma a girl and her family have to undergo when a boy posts digitally manipulated pictures of her on the Internet, falsely implicating her in an illicit relationship with a man. Speaking about it, she shared:

> The realisation of hurting someone's feelings, that is not there anymore … This is a true story about a family that's based in

Karachi; the characters I've written about are all in Karachi, and the interesting thing is that *Pakeeza* also reaches [the boy's] home. The monthly sketches of domestic comedy *Jaltarang* [Jingling Music] are also drawn from stories women tell me on the phone. One would say, 'There was an outfit my husband didn't like, so I gave it to my mother-in-law'. Or another would say, 'My sister-in-law has such an evil eye, our new car became dented the day we went over to see her'. So all this provides me material for my sketches.[4]

In some sense, it was understandable why women wanted to share their stories with her. There was a particular sense of support that her tone conveyed. 'May they become your strength just as you are their strength' was the touching response when I answered a question about my children. There was also a familiar, familial tone to the conversation; writing and relations were entwined. Towards the end of the conversation, I congratulated her on her son's wedding. He had recently married a girl who studied with him in Australia. Photographs and details of the reception had been published in the magazine and were public. 'When I saw my son at the airport, I began crying … I'm now trying to find a girl for my other son: do you know of any [Pakistani] girls in Australia or America?' At the time, her anecdotes about her family sounded peripheral—something that was not central—but increasingly this excess became a large part of the story. Relations and feelings about those relations were not comfort-generating conversation pluggers but defined the very bonds of this community. Moreover, this sharing took an affective form. As quoted earlier, Ansar did not simply share that her son had arrived but also how the arrival had affected her emotionally. This form also continued to shimmer throughout the rest of the conversations. In this context, I was also expected to share emotionally and not just factually.

I began to notice this as I concluded an interview. 'But you haven't told me about yourself.' In response to this now familiar closing question, I reiterated facts I had provided more or less at the beginning of the conversation: ethnically half Pakhtun and half

Punjabi, raised in Islamabad, single parent to two boys, currently studying in the United States. However, the sense that the invitation was to share something else nagged at me. I began to sense that the question was not about what my life was like or how I positioned myself, but rather about how I felt about living my life.

Let me share another phone call to explain this. The answers this writer gave also interwove familial relations into her life. Even factual questions, such as where she wrote, elicited responses that shone with personal and familial detail.

> When I began writing, my parents were alive, so I would just sit anywhere with my register and start writing. My mother would bring me everything [to eat or drink] wherever I was sitting [*har cheez mujh tak pohanch jati thi*]. My speed was such that I would write a short story in one sitting, one day, but now it's different. [Pausing] I have two younger sisters; they are both married but take care of me like mothers do. [Rapidly] May God always keep them happy and give them a long life—but of course, it's not the same. I am now working with AB Productions, but my speed isn't what it was.[5]

The opening line, 'When I began writing, my parents were alive', drew an unfamiliar link. Where she wrote was inextricably linked with the absence of her parents and how that affected her. Writing was not simply writing in itself, and the phone conversation was not merely to provide information about herself. Perhaps it was an encounter that was expected to establish a relationship, and the avenue toward that relationship was through sharing her world. Not just facts about family, people around her who were important to her, but perhaps more important was her inner world and its mood and concerns. During the first few minutes of my phone call, as I waited for her, I could hear the sounds of her home: news channel on the television, her voice giving instructions on what needed to be done in the kitchen, finally, an exasperated 'Ibraheem' as she picked up the phone. Her tone mirrored the memory of my own exasperation as my toddlers ran to the phone and grabbed it before I could. I thought of sharing that my son was also named Ibraheem, but didn't. At that time, I had justified that decision by thinking this might seem like hierarchical social positioning. I wasn't sure whether she was married or not, or if she had any children, so I didn't want to go in that direction. However, this holding back went deeper. I was placing myself as an academic; presenting myself to them in a certain way that I hoped would evoke trust. Yet deep down I was not willing to show my emotional side, what concerned me, what moved me, and reciprocate the level of trust I expected from them. Even the placing of facts was careful and deliberate. The fact of studying and living in the United States was positioned after that of being on study leave from a university in Islamabad.

Gradually, this began to change. The philosopher John Llewelyn's (2012) words, 'The space between us dilates, it opens and closes with affect', come to mind as I think of the next phone call.[6] Early in the morning, as I sat writing last night's interview with a writer who is now famous in the world of television, I heard my mother's excited voice behind me. 'You spoke for such a long time. What's she like, what does she sound like? I mean, what is her voice like? Raheela (fictitious name) spoke with you for such a long time.' I thought of the joke we had shared about being given special attention at home today because of this interview. This is when I realised that part of the difficulty in terms of writing it now was that of stance. Gearing up for the interview, as I saw 'Call me after 9 p.m.' flashing on the mobile phone, I had positioned myself as an academic, interviewing a prolific writer. Not yet forty, she had written over fifteen books and numerous short stories and TV scripts. Regardless of the form it took, her writing was extremely popular in Pakistan. Moreover, she was a public yet private figure. Her work and writings are well known, as are the basic contours of her life (institutions studied or worked in, the city she lives in, and her age and date of birth). She is also accessible through her mobile phone number. But there are few photos of her on the Internet or in magazines. This then overturns the dynamic of celebrities being known visually but being inaccessible in terms of a one-to-one conversation.[7]

'What would she sound like? I hope I can get an early date for a meeting with her', were the thoughts that flashed through my mind as I dialled her number. I heard a leisurely paced 'Hello'.

'Thank you for giving me your time; I know you're very busy.'

'That's okay. Everyone's time is precious. You've also taken time out from your schedule to speak to me.'

Realising that I could not simply drive over in the morning to her place as I had planned, because she was not currently in her home town, was disappointing. 'Yet another fieldworking rhythm that I hadn't anticipated,' I thought to myself. Shifting gears, I asked her if I could ask a few questions over the phone. Three hours and three disconnections later, I found myself speaking to her as I would to a friend. Somewhere during the course of that phone call, the solid binaries of the aura of this writer's reputation and my concerns about conducting an interview the right way had become fluid. It became a conversation with Raheela rather than an interview of Raheela Ahmed.

What led to this dynamic? Was it the closeness in age or the familiarity with her work? Alternatively, was it the fact that it was a late-night conversation, which has its own intimacy and easy spaces for self-disclosure? Unanswered thoughts. Although Raheela did not mention a specific number in terms of daily phone calls; long conversations seemed to be usual for her. The disconnections were puzzling until she explained that this was usual; every sixty minutes the mobile phone call gets disconnected and has to be re-dialled. Even her birthday sounded like a never-ending stream of phone calls and text messages. 'No, it doesn't tire me. I know that I have it now [referring to her fame], but after a few years, I may not have it anymore.' The apparent contradiction between her being an intensely private person yet a very welcoming listener became more understandable when she spoke about the way readers wanted to share their lives:

> I don't like to appear in public or have my photos on the Internet. But also it's because when people—readers—approach me, it's usually to share something from their life, not really to know something about mine. Teenagers, for instance, call me, and I know they must have gone to great lengths to get my number. When they call, they want to share problems that they're encountering and can't share with others. These days, it's a tragedy, but most people find it difficult to share problems with their family, parents, or siblings; in some way it's easier for them to talk to me about it. I think [it is] also because I already know everything there is to know about myself. People assume that I don't talk about my life because I have something to hide, but it's just because I'm bored. I want to learn about other people—why would I keep talking about myself?

A few months later, as I watched her televised play on YouTube, I heard a character say, 'Ami [mother], I've stood eighteenth in the CSS [Civil Superior Services] exam'. There was a childish pleasure in wondering if she had drawn this from our conversation when I'd spoken about a friend who'd stood eighteenth in the same exam.

At one level, in this world of writers and readers, my position was that of a reader and a journalist-like figure who wanted to know more about these writers and editors. The identity as a reader became more prominent as I was heard and that of a journalist as I was seen. There was a discernible difference based on how the interview was conducted. Ethnographically, I was expected to follow the daily rhythms of the people who had allowed me into their lives. However, for these women, being a writer was a private activity. As some of them shared, when they began writing, they did not disclose this to their families. Given the social position of this genre as lowbrow, frivolous fiction, it is not well respected; thus, most writers hid this from the family and friends. In some ways this was an intensely private activity for these writers, and

the presence of their family and the roles they had to play as a host/
mother/wife when I visited them at home affected the interview
process.

Going to their homes, I was able to meet them in person and see
their living environment. Yet as I walked to their doorway, they
received me as a host and positioned me as a guest with certain
markers of age and class. In their home I would speak to them
in the sitting room, usually referred to as the drawing room (the
room reserved for entertaining guests), record, and leave after
a while. The time they gave me was also that when guests are
usually received: ten or eleven in the morning or four or five in the
afternoon. Information about their writing was interwoven with
taking care of my needs (for instance, noticing if I had finished my
drink and wanted another). Family members trailed in and out of
the room, sometimes reminding the writer to relate some specific
detail about an award or a special number (issue of a magazine that
had been dedicated to that writer). I was placed as a journalist but
not really a reader, as readers rarely visit writers at home. After the
first meeting, they would remain in touch over the phone, often
calling to chat or ask about other writers I had met, but invitations
to visit again were not extended.

Phone conversations, on the other hand, seemed to lead to
greater self-disclosure and ease. Thus, here the usual sociality
of being available for meeting in person rather than over the
phone was upturned. The body became a hindrance. Arriving at
someone's home, it had to be placed (in the drawing room), and it
needed to be tended to (food, tea, water). The way the body arrived
(cab, car, rickshaw) or was dressed also brought into play a certain
sociality of class.[8] The writers whom I visited at home were very
warm and welcoming, but there was a dynamic of intimacy and
ease which was particular to phone conversations, therefore the
invitation to share feelings about my own life: 'You haven't told me
about yourself'—not really facts but a certain kind of emotional
sharing of facts.

EMOTIONAL RESONANCE

This blurring between facts and feelings about those facts was perhaps the most prominent in the phone conversation with a senior writer with over 450 stories to her name. My initial phone call received an unexpected call back and an apology for not answering the phone. I told her I was interviewing digest writers and wanted to talk to her about her writing, and I would use this interview for the paper I was going to write about the digest community. She said she had to prepare lunch, but we could talk in the evening.

In response to a question about herself, she began by speaking about her childhood. 'I don't know if I should be telling you this, but I was adopted by my *khala* [mother's sister] when I was two years and four months old [*sava do saal*]. [Pausing] Will you write this in your interview?'

'It's up to you; if you don't want me to write it, I won't.' I thought of other instances in which writers had told me not to transcribe something; the unambiguous tone they had adopted was not here this time. Moreover, rather than the general term *bachpan* (childhood), she had given an exact age, '*sava do saal*', which suggested this was an important turning point in her mental landscape.

'No, it's okay, you can write it. [Hesitantly] Tell me again, this interview is for …?'

'It's for my studies, and I will use it for the thesis.' Her '*achha*' (akin to the English expression 'Okay!') prompted me to continue. But continue how? She wanted to hear more, and somehow this more was not really about confidentiality or circulation of the information. The moment outlined here was one where I could sense that something significant was happening but did not really know what it was or the direction it was taking. Perhaps more than anything else, there was a notion that her question and our interaction were not a matter of communication but of connection. The anthropologist John Dewsbury (2003) identifies these ethnographic moments that 'arrive unannounced' as ones in which we have a sense that something is present in which we believe, even though we cannot comprehend it in any tangible way. He suggests that the intensity of these moments is similar to the intensity of a work of art or the sensations of a dance. They communicate their own meaning, but that meaning is different from the register or filter to which we are accustomed. In such cases the presenter cannot present meaning; not 'what happens' but 'it happens'.

This was one such moment, and I found myself mirroring her tone. In some sense, the tone led to words: words about calling from Islamabad, where I was living with my mother, my worries about her health, and my father's death from a brain tumour. I paused as my mind wandered to the last few days of his life when he could no longer recognise faces. I heard her voice again; this time, the hesitant tone was replaced with an intimate, quiet note.

> No, that's okay. So I was adopted by my aunt and only came back to live with my own mother later, I insisted because I missed her too much. In Karachi, my mother would come to visit me, and I would call her *khala* and call my aunt *ami*. When they would both be sitting together, I would ignore my own mother and keep talking to my aunt. But then I decided I wanted to go back to my mother. So I think there was hurt inside me [*sic*]. I suffered the pain of separation [*vichoray ka dard*] at a very young age, being separated from my mother. Writers write because they have some pain inside them, and this was my pain. Even now, when I write stories, I find myself placing the girl either in her uncle's house or aunt's house; she's usually not living with her parents, so this is something deep inside me that comes out from within me. I moved back, but after two and a half years, my mother passed away.

It is uncertain what she was establishing and I was unsure whether my response was the correct one. What does stand out is that it was something similar to an intimate feeling rather than an intimate fact. The fact of being adopted was shared easily, but the sharing of feelings about that fact required a particular form of emotional knowledge. Thus, trust was predicated on a certain form of emotional resonance.

This emotional resonance is similar to what the literary theorist Lauren Berlant identifies as shared experiential knowledge 'in each other's experience of power, intimacy, desire, and discontent, with all that entails' (Berlant, 2008: 5).[9] Berlant suggests that abstract notions such as nation or public attain authority or legitimacy through the affective engagement people have with these identities. She particularly focuses on the public sphere which both surrounds and grows from media, such as these digests, geared toward women. Marginalised groups, such as women, form an intimate public which has its own processes of identification and engagement. This public is not intimate on the basis of autobiographical sharing as such but because 'consumers of its particular stuff already share a worldview and emotional knowledge that they have derived from a broadly common historical experience' (Berlant, 2008: vii). Thus, rather than women simply identifying with one another's longings or empathising with one another's sufferings, it is a form of relationality with its own processes of engagement. Thus, life stories are shared, but there are particular norms of engagement and initiatives predicated on sensing whether these narratives resonate with the other: feelings about family and relatives, obligations and their effect on the writing process, a particular form of humour that entails familiarity with the digest's idiomatic language, and a shared sense of being connected. Perhaps they are connected as women, or maybe connected as women at a particular juncture in time within the social milieu of Pakistani society, or, more specifically, connected to the digest community. In this way, life stories are shared easily, but there is also the dynamic of the person sensing and judging if her inner world finds resonance with the listener.

The writers with whom I had phone conversations also extended emotional contact and shared text messages. The text messages began slowly and increased steadily. Initially, this was an avenue to contact writers and ask for a good time to call them. Messages from writers began trickling in when they sent contact numbers of other writers I had asked for. 'Dear, I think you should talk to this other writer also,' some of them helpfully added. Gradually, they changed to a spontaneous daily checking in: 'Congratulations, you have become a celebrity☺, check your news in this month's *Pakeeza*'; 'Got your emails [referring to consent forms for respondents] wishing you all the luck with your surgery dear. And get well soon☺'.[10] On other occasions, the text messages were in the form of a particular kind of knowing and sharing. They brought out aspects of the conversation we had just had. In such cases, the conversation did not end with the phone call. The mobile phone would beep as texts in Roman Urdu (transliteration of Urdu) flashed on the screen. Increasingly, I found myself reaching out for the mobile as soon as I opened my eyes in the morning to check whether there was a message from a writer. Each had her own rhythm and pattern. One writer sent her text messages at three or four in the morning (when she woke up), witty one-liners commenting on something that had happened during the previous day; another sent texts late in the afternoon, usually with numbers of other writers she felt I should contact. Two others sent messages that were in the form of letters.

The memory of an evening floats back. I was sitting in the darkened sitting room playing back and recording a phone interview when a text message arrived:

It was good to talk to you, even though I still feel there are more conversations to be covered. I belong to the spiritual family of Sindh. Sindh has always been the centre of love, spirituality and peace, but the feudals have tried to mutilate it through illiteracy and poverty, Sindh's resources surpass its problems. However the indifference of rulers and the plunder of government machinery/ system have made rich Sindh a poor Sindh. I have tried my best for a school in my area, so that the children can get a scholarship and can at least join a school in the nearby city. The financial situation of the people of my village is not good. It is not that people are against education; they don't have the finances for it. The non-government schools, it costs a lot to get children educated there. How can people who are worried about their next meal spend Rs. 3,000—4,000 on education? You haven't told me about yourself, about your family etc. I hope that you will be very successful in your academics. Amen. If life continues, companionship will too [*Yaar zinda suhbat baqi*]. [11]

This could be viewed as an indirect invitation for financial help for the charity school in the village. However, the message was written in Roman Urdu—each letter of the alphabet punched in individually, rather than the quicker, more efficient, edit option that can be used for English words. Therefore, the time and effort she had put into this message was a reflection not just of her humanity but also a particular kind of attunement to a world that has opened up through sound waves.

Another writer, who had gone on to television script writing, gave a similar example of how a text message from a reader had led her to feel an 'emotional pull' towards the community of digest readers.

In some sense the emotional pull is very strong for me too. I had decided that I would not go back to digest writing after I had started writing for television. My decision was reversed by a text message sent by a young girl. She had written that she had tears in her eyes because seeing my plays on air, she felt she had lost me to this other world. I then realised that for many women, television or even the books that are published are simply not accessible. The only access to fiction or writing they can afford is the 50–60 rupee [$0.50] digest. This is why I decided to go back to digest writing [with my current serialised novel]. [12]

There is sociability between women with its own sensory feel of rhythm and sound. There are no isolated chunks of time as such—daily life remains in, and conversations weave around, the rhythm of daily routines: 'Call me after 9 p.m.', 'Give me a minute, I need to turn off the stove'. In one instance a writer explained that she could not communicate late at night the family slept outside because of long power breakdowns (commonly called load-shedding). Because voice carries far, it is more comfortable to talk at five in the evening when she's done with her chores but is inside and can converse.

As a reader or writer dials or answers a call, what is she doing at that precise moment, for whom, and for what? Is it an attunement to a world where they have the freedom to be present yet absent? What do they witness about themselves as they speak to a woman who has never seen them and whom they will probably never see? There are no definite answers to these questions, but what is certain is that the world of readers and writers is one that operates through sound waves and text messages travelling over mobile phones.

It is then a 'public face of anonymity, a transient coming together of people unconnected by relations of kin, religion, or ethnicity' (Larkin, 2002: 324). In this way, voices become just that: voices that exchange life stories and experiences.[13]

To reiterate, the previous section is drawn from my initial encounters with digest writers. It highlights my position as a researcher and my assumption that sharing information about my life would suffice to draw me into this community. This assumption proved erroneous, as conversations with the writers entailed a willingness to share feelings about my life rather than just facts about it. I contrast this level of intimacy with the experience of interviewing writers at home and point out that there was a discernible difference in the interviews conducted over the phone and in person. The writers I met in person were very warm and welcoming, but the social parameters of being a guest led to a somewhat superficial exchange. More meetings, of course, carried the promise of deeper trust but I find it significant that phone conversations carried this dynamic from the very outset.

The next section elaborates on the absence of ethnic and political identities in this sound community and delineates bonds formed in subgroups.

BONDS IN A WORLD OF INVISIBLE ETHNIC AND POLITICAL IDENTITIES

The news headlines this morning (6 August 2015) inform us of military courts being deemed legal by the Supreme Court, water levels in certain dams rising to dangerous levels, and how increasingly, highly educated professionals appear to be becoming members of extremist groups.[14] My point in setting out these issues is to highlight the sense of being on the brink, which usually permeates daily life in Pakistan. This is accompanied by the belief that there is an ideological current that needs to be corrected and manoeuvred in the right direction—toward safety and stability. Thus, headlines are not just news updates but carry an urgency and emotional weight.

Party affiliations are openly shared, loudly discussed, and sometimes changed as disillusionment sets in. However, in the digest public, there is an implicit social etiquette of not discussing 'politics' in the sense of political loyalties towards a certain party or explicit critique of government policies. As a matter of policy, political affiliations are silenced in digest stories. Even sentences that hint at a writer's political affiliations are censored. For instance, a writer shared that an episode of her novel hinted at the 2006 Red Mosque incident. In this case, a group of madrassa students took over a children's library. This escalated into a clash between madrassa students and the government, culminating in an army operation leading to the death of numerous women and children. Public opinion was divided, as some saw the action as an essential step in establishing the writ of the state while others saw it as needless killing. The sense of sorrow and grief over lost lives of army personnel as well as madrassa students was published in the digest story. However, the line 'What happened inside the mosque was wrong, but what happened outside it was equally wrong', was censored.[15]

During 2014 and 2015, numerous incidents of political, ethnic, and religious violence took place. Of these, only one was given space in digest editorials and letters sections: the murder of over 134 schoolchildren by the Taliban in December 2014. However, in this case too, rather than a critique of policy, as the national outpouring of grief in mainstream media entailed, digest editorials and letters focused on the sense of sadness and loss.

> As we watched the photos [of the young boys] on television, my daughter, my daughter-in-law, and myself, all three of us had tears running down our faces. One looked so carefree, another was posing like a hero.[16]

Even in times of political division, this culture of silence continues. For instance, in August 2014, two national political parties organised a sit-in in the capital city of Islamabad to demonstrate against the government. This continued for four months, and everyday conversations often became aggressive as well as divisive. Trivial comments, such as complaints about road blockages that the sit-in had led to, would often snowball into aggressive arguments. Even visits to spaces such as hair salons entailed divisive dichotomies, as women would often ask whether one was attending the sit-in. Even so, when I interacted with various editors and writers, I was never asked my views about this situation, even though personal details of my life, such as whether my pay would increase after completing a PhD, or how I felt about my ex-husband, were easily asked. In this sense, there is an overturning of the public and private. The issues that are usually visible and public, such as one's ethnic or political affiliation, remain in the background, whereas issues or sentiments that are usually regarded as personal and private are publicly shared.

A brief explanation of the productive dimensions of censorship is necessary here to contextualise my argument. Censorship is usually viewed as restrictive but also has its productive dimension. Indeed, scholars such as Bourdieu (1991) and Butler (1997, 1998) suggest that censorship is a precondition for subjectivity itself, and the very possibility of agency in language depends upon a foreclosure. To take a very simple example, as we use *I*, we simultaneously negate *you* and *we* so it becomes intelligible as *not you, not them—not us*. In this sense, each configuration becomes intelligible through the various possibilities that are disavowed. Building on this, anthropologists Kaur and Mazzarella (2009) state that rather than being dominant over the public sphere, censorship is both in and of it. In other words, censorship is subject to public scrutiny and is often intertwined with publicity (for instance, books that are banned often receive greater publicity than if they had not been banned). Moreover, censorship is actually dependent upon objectionable material, both structurally and sensuously. Structurally, it is dependent in the sense that if there were nothing to censor, censorship would cease to exist; sensuously, it is dependent because no one other than the censors pays as much attention to the provocative word or image. In this context, rather than a simple process of silencing, censorship can be 'read as a relentless proliferation of discourses on normative modes of desiring, of acting, of being in the world' (Kaur and Mazzarella, 2009: 5). Thus, the matter is not a simple one of domination or silencing but a curious entanglement that simultaneously leads to several different processes.

This framework is useful for our purpose, as editorial censorship policies have led to a particular culture in this community where ethnic and political divisions become insignificant. Fear of violent reaction by political parties or the state obliges editors to steer clear of the political or ethnic turmoil that is a usual part of daily life in Pakistan. However, this policy has led to a particular dynamic where an individual's identity as a reader or writer is predicated on her/his views about relationships and morality rather than ethnic or political loyalties. Therefore, bonds are formed through shared feelings rather than shared political and/or ethnic affiliations, but this is not as such a conscious effort.

Let us now trace varying forms of support and emotional sharing within subgroups of writers. I had often heard of Ayesha from another writer, Simran (fictitious names). 'She actually called up another writer to ask her to talk to the production house to increase my rate.' 'She gets worried over little things, like she was confused about the smell in her room, and we finally figured out it came from the wet towel under her bed.' Ayesha was initially a reader and then gradually began to write stories too. In this context, she began to contact some other writers whose work she liked. Over time she became close to two writers, Raheela and Simran, and they became familiar with one another's families, daily routines, and relationships. The texture of her conversations with each varied from the trivial to the problematic. She had never met any of these writers because they both lived in different provinces of Pakistan; nonetheless, the bond continued to grow.

Simran, who had also been conversing regularly with Ayesha's mother, felt particularly responsible for Ayesha's wellbeing after her mother passed away. She maintained regular contact, occasionally calling up to six times a day to ensure that Ayesha was not feeling lonely. One evening, Simran called me to express her concerns about Ayesha, whose fiancé had suddenly ended their engagement. As Ayesha lacked family support, Simran called this man, who is based overseas, and shared with me. 'I thought he feels he can get away with it because Ayesha's parents are not alive anymore, so I wanted to make sure he knows she has people who support and care for her.'

Raheela also offered to speak to him, but Ayesha refused because she felt that given this writer's personality, Raheela would be too hard on him, and she might lose any prospects of mending the relationship. When Raheela sensed her hesitation, she instead offered to help her by using her contacts to place her in a women's hostel. As Ayesha told me of this writer's efforts, she shared that she had initially not told her about her personal problems. However, one day, as Raheela called Ayesha, she heard her sibling shouting in the background and began to realise her situation. Subsequently, she helped Ayesha become financially independent through script writing. Therefore, in terms of both achieving financial independence and receiving emotional support, the unseen community of writers became her anchor.

Ayesha's bond with Simran and Raheela began because their stories resonated with her, which led to her efforts to approach them and cultivate a relationship. This in turn led to a relationship that provided practical support and daily contact, filling the vacuum caused by an absent family. Support and practical help such as this are commonplace. To take another example, one afternoon a writer called me from Pakistan to ask if I knew a Pukhtoon family based near my home town in the US. She then explained that a reader's mother-in-law was harassing her. As the writer described this girl's plight, there was also a sense of practical 'doing' in terms of whether I knew anyone in her husband's family or the institution where he worked.

Similarly, during a conversation, Simran began discussing her experience of working with Raheela on script writing. Being asthmatic, Simran often suffers from breathing problems. Once she felt so ill that she decided she could not work any longer. She, therefore, texted Raheela and told her to find another junior writer to work on the script. When Raheela learnt about Simran's illness and the pain she was suffering, she continued to send text messages. Simran explained that it was two in the morning when she texted. Raheela had discerned that at that time Simran's family members were asleep, and she was alone in experiencing the fear and discomfort that accompany breathing problems. She also realised that it was difficult for Simran to talk, so rather than calling, she continued to send text messages for the next few hours till it was morning and Simran's family members were awake.

As I look back, what stands out the most is the easy manner in which these gestures were shared. I see them as extraordinary, but for the women who shared these gestures, it appeared to be an ordinary dynamic that accompanied these relationships. My point is that at one level, these are ordinary instances of emotional support that often form part of friendship, yet at another level they are extraordinary because this support is extended between women who rarely ever meet one another.

Let us now turn to questions such as how this trust functions and what sustains it. What constitutes normality here in terms of daily practices, and what ruptures or unsettles these bonds?

Trust

Like any other relationship, these bonds too progress through different moments which gradually build trust. Conversations usually begin because a reader likes a writers' work and finds emotional resonance with it. The story is the identity marker, a window into how a writer sees the world. Some writers are good conversationalists and can relate easily; others cannot. Therefore, depending upon whether the emotional connection is present or absent, the interaction continues. Sentences such as 'I've liked talking to you' often accompany the initial conversation as a form of signal that the conversation was meaningful and there is a desire to continue the interaction. Women also call other women who are readers based on common identification or bond with a writer. In such cases too, the relationship is predicated on a kind of emotional contact and sharing.

Let us briefly turn to an ethnographic example to draw certain contours of this dynamic. During a particularly difficult phase in Ayesha's life, Simran told me that the former needed some information about the US visa process. That evening when Ayesha called me, our first conversation extended to over three hours. The visa process formed a minor part of it, but the larger dynamics of problems in her family relationships and a sharing of her inner world formed the primary texture of our interaction. As I highlighted in an earlier section, facts about her life were not significant, but what was is how she felt about those facts.

There are, of course, personality differences that establish how much one shares about their personal life. My point, however, is that in Ayesha's case, it was safer to disclose all she did and share her feelings because I had no connection with her family or workplace. Ayesha and I did share a network of common acquaintances in the digest community, and therefore there was the slight risk of this private sharing becoming public gossip. However, the notions of family respectability or portraying a certain sense of stability as an individual's work persona that such networks usually entail were absent. In this sense, lack of physical proximity and the absence of visual cues led to the form of anonymity where emotions could be safely shared.

There is then an intermingling of practical help (arranging for accommodation, talking to a problematic fiancé) and attunement to emotional sharing that are facilitated through physical distance and absence of visual cues of class, age, and social background. Moreover, the long conversation with Ayesha—listening to her concerns and feelings—did not feel like an obligation; it was similar to the experience of reading a digest story and entering another person's inner world.

Let us first explore what 'inner world' might mean here. Fiction, whether in print or electronic, is predicated on a suspension of disbelief. However, as Radway (1984) states, whereas the electronic medium (television or cinema) is usually a public, social, or familial experience, the activity of reading entails a private experiencing of emotions. In other words, watching television is a social activity in that it is often undertaken in the presence of others, influenced by the preferences of other family members. It permits both simultaneous conversation and personal interaction. Silent reading, on the other hand, is a private activity, as it requires the reader to block out her surroundings. In this sense, the reader enters another world with fictional companionship and conversation, where feelings can be privately experienced. In this framework, reading a digest story entails both a suspension of disbelief and emotional contact with the inner worlds that are being shared by other women through their fiction. The scenes of domesticity, problems in relationships, and everyday dilemmas are different in each story but similar in terms of the broader familiarity of daily life in Pakistan as middle-class women. Thus, the sensibility of emotional connection, trust, and suspension of disbelief developed through reading digest stories by other women appears to carry over to conversations over the phone as well.

Let us now turn to ruptures in these relationships. An unspoken understanding is that these ties are predicated on sincerity and an emotional connect rather than any ulterior motive. Instrumentality constitutes a rupture. Normality is breached when a writer uses these bonds for some other purpose and violates this norm of being in touch for its own sake. I was often told how a popular writer had used these relationships to further her own career. The variety of people who shared this with me (writers in different subgroups as well as an editor) and the tone of its narration indicated its significance. Initially, she used to call senior writers frequently to talk to them to avail assistance for her stories, 'at all times of day and night'. Then, once she became well known, her attitude changed. She refused to accept the phone calls of those who had helped her. She was therefore viewed as having used these relationships to further her own career and discarded them once she had achieved fame. As one writer said, 'She is like a small utensil that is unsteadied as it brims over (with fame or success)'. Her writing was not criticised but her exploitation of bonds in the sound sensorium marked her as an outsider—as someone whose inner nature (*fitrat*) did not match the norm.

There are also occasional cases of deception. These usually involve a man posing as a woman. For instance, an editor's spouse began to reply to text messages sent by digest readers. However, as they were accustomed to the words she used and her tone and personality in text messages, they sensed someone was posing as her. As one writer shared, 'Like, she doesn't open up too much, but that time she was asking, "So tell me more, etc." and I thought, this is not her but her husband posing, so I just said, "I'll call you at the office", and ended it.' Given the close interaction within this community, this news travelled rapidly, and other women became watchful about messaging that editor. In fact, as I expressed my wish to interview this man, I was also cautioned not to use my own number, as he could become clingy (*chipkoo*).

Through this example, let us transition to how these relationships interact with marital and familial bonds.

Interaction with Familial Bonds

Familial responsibilities take precedence, and conversations weave around the daily tasks of cooking or taking care of children. When you are needed as a family member, these conversations take a back seat. News of family (wedding, death) is shared but with the implicit understanding that the person might not be available. For instance, when Simran's father passed away, the news was shared over text messages ('I wanted to tell you Simran's baba has passed away, her Telenor number is off but you can leave a message at the Ufone one'). During the first few days when she kept her phone off or on silent, it was understood that her responsibilities as a daughter were more important than such communication. She later replied to missed calls and text messages with an explanation that she would call back when she was ready. This was easily understood and accepted. There was an implicit understanding that her familial responsibilities needed to take precedence at this point, and therefore digest friendships were paused and later resumed once her extended family had left. Similarly, when a writer lost two of her sisters to an unexpected illness, the news was shared in close subgroups but with a reminder that she did not want the news to be circulated. Thus, other writers and readers and I continued to speak to her without raising the subject unless she did so herself.

Family relationships are often discussed, but in the context of sentiments about them or through minor domestic details. The usual questions about a person's husband's or father's employment, common in the Pakistani context, are not vocalised here. You might learn about what someone's husband said about text messages or the kind of food he liked, but details of institutional employment frequently remain private. This dynamic is also reflected in the marriage news column, where a reader or a writer narrates the details of a wedding. Trivialities such as a child's temper tantrum or power breakdowns form a usual part of the narrative but facts regarding the groom's employment or religious affiliations are absent.

The textured sentimentality of phone conversations, an emphasis on emotions, also figures in the narration of family events in digests. News of a family member's illness is accompanied by expressions of concern and anxiety. Death of a family member is also shared within the framework of emotions relating to it. Facts about what that family member did during their life are sometimes added, but the emotions take precedence.

This co-mingling of shared and unshared is also present in terms of what family members know of a writer's closeness to another writer or reader. The person on the phone is not a mysterious X but someone whom the family indirectly knows. Conversations follow a certain rhythm that weaves around the daily routine. Family members are familiar with this and aware of the closeness. Occasionally, a younger sister or child might also pick up the phone to have a conversation. The voice of the caller, broad (or trivial) details of her life, and the daily rhythms of these conversations are usually known by family members. However, what is discussed in the conversations, whether it is playful banter or sombre, confidential problems, is not shared. Most writers have an emotional investment in maintaining the relationships formed with other digest writers or readers. They, therefore, share certain details to make the person known or public to their family members and maintain a visible openness about the friendship. However, the emotional intimacy of the relationship remains intact, as conversations usually take place in private.

Both family members and friends, in a sense, become fictional characters. Given the absence of physical proximity, whatever is known of a woman's family comes only through the woman herself. Similarly, family members' opinions about a friend depend upon how a woman chooses to portray her. In other words, life at home and varying shades of familial relationships (sombre or lively) are created through conversations. A family's openness about the friendship is also created through a certain portrayal of the unseen friend. A sculpting of her character that facilitates familial approval ensures that the conversations will continue.

Let us now move from snapshots to the specific forms this emotional connection can take by tracing the ethnographic experience of being in a dyad with a writer.

EMOTIONAL LEANING IN A DYAD

I had phone interviews with a writer, whom we will call Simran, during the initial phase of my fieldwork in 2012 and 2013. However, our daily interaction began when I returned to Pakistan in the summer of 2014. This was a vulnerable time; I was beginning to experience doubts about whether I would be able to get anything done. Unlike most other graduate friends who had a central, physical space for fieldwork (a mall, a neighbourhood), I had, so to say, no space to cast anchor. There were no lively readers' groups or a digest office in or even near the city in which I lived. Thus, my daily interaction (and additions to field notes) was primarily dependent on the time individual writers and readers took out from their personal schedules.

It was comforting to think that I lived as they did, within the daily realm of familial relationships, digest narratives, and long-term, personal investment in what was happening in Pakistan.[17] Yet, at another level, the fragility of daily bonds and fieldwork being predicated on this contact was disconcerting. Relationships are easily formed through phone conversations, but are just as easily ruptured. A reader or a writer might take a call and converse, but they are just as free to stop taking calls. An additional problem was the suspicion some digest writers had over my association with the US. Prevalent perceptions about US involvement in Pakistan's national affairs fuelled this suspicion. To reiterate, as the anthropologist Patricia Zavella (2003) suggests, as 'insider researchers', often what we find relevant about our identity, or what we assume the respondents relate to as common ground, might be very different from how the respondents perceive us. For instance, in her case, she expected her Chicana identity to be relevant in her research with working-class Chicana women. However, her respondents positioned her as an educated and privileged woman rather than a Chicana like them.

Similarly, my Pakistani identity helped here but I was also positioned as being affiliated with the US and often asked sceptical questions such as: why would the US want to study digest writers? In this context, each time a writer did not pick up the phone, I often wondered whether it was due to a loss of trust or simply a matter of being preoccupied. Various doubts nagged at me and pulled me down: 'How will I get this done? Will this even qualify as ethnography?' However, I began realising that each exploration has its own life. It does not need my steering because it has its own flow. Thus, whatever needs to be told will emerge if I remain open and relinquish the need to control.

With this frame of mind, I called up Simran. She warmly welcomed me back—'Where had you disappeared to?'—and began updating me on her family news. The conversation flowed, and toward the end, she quietly recalled our last conversation. 'You had asked me towards the end why my stories had such sadness.'

After I put down the phone, the screen kept flashing through various text messages that flowed.

S: I have really enjoyed talking to you.
K: So have I.
S: Isn't it good when we experience something as being good.
K: Being good is also very good.
S: Those who [make us feel good] live in our hearts and are nearer to us than those who live near us.

Gradually, this banter became a regular part of the day. Text messages were also accompanied by a certain sense of being there and sharing each other's lives. For instance, one evening as I sat in front of the sputtering gas heater organising my notes for the day, I noticed the phone screen flashing with an incoming text message from Simran. 'My niece is pretending to be Dracula, I'm acting scared, and she's giggling.' 'Now she's pulling my cheeks and telling me I'm her baby.'

Not only did her presence calm my doubts about fieldwork, there was also a sense of being heard, an emotional leaning that I began wondering about. The friendship progressed through moments of knowing and being known, a certain play of light-heartedness, heavy-heartedness, and intimacy which were carried through explicit expressions of treasuring the other person.

Let me share an extract from my notes at the time, followed by a description of a typical day.

The only consistent thread here so far have been my conversations with Simran; we talk every night for an hour or so. She has seen my photo and I've seen hers. Last night she was telling me about her friend Sameen, about an editor, about two other writers, and about her day. I also learnt how her favourite part of the house is a wood structure up on the roof where she spends most of her day. Her familial references are now all clear: her brother Fayzan who loves eating, her brother Sarmad who takes a lot of photos, her father and his usual gestures of bringing pastries for her each time he comes home from travel to the nearby city. [sic]

As I opened my eyes in the morning to turn off the alarm on my phone, I would find several texts she had sent during the night. I would reply to them and then work till it was time to take the children to school. Around 11 a.m. or so, when she woke up, she would text to check if I was free. Either she would call or I would, depending upon who had free minutes (free call time offered by telecom companies during specific hours) at the time. The familiar morning sounds of her home accompanied her voice: her sister telling her tea was ready, her chattering nieces ('Look at me! What is this?'), and Simran's exclamations ('Be careful, be careful') as they ran down the stairs or jumped around.

For instance, in one conversation I began by telling her about a function I had attended the previous evening and what it had felt like to encounter someone I had broken up with a long time ago. Simran shared her confusion about whether she should remain in touch with a friend's sister-in-law who was also a writer. The conversation then turned to what had to be done during the day. For me, the morning entailed a trip to the bank, an interview with a writer, and bringing my children home from school. Simran planned aloud her discussion with an editor and the days she had left for sending the next episode of her novel. Intermittent text messages communicating either what each was doing at the time or a shared thought continued in the evening till a late-night conversation.[18] As we became familiar with each other's emotional landscapes, family members, and romantic relationships, anecdotes about her friend Sameen (fictitious name) became a recurring pattern in our conversation.

As I begin writing about Sameen, my recent conversation with Simran comes to mind. Last evening, when I was walking in the park, Simran called and asked her usual question: 'Which chapter are you writing now?'

'Yours and Sameen's, but I don't know how to bring out the feel of it, or even where to begin.'

I had spent a frustrating morning trying to organise points for this section, but each framing felt inadequate. Simran carefully listened and replied, 'Why don't you start with that conversation about the moon, the one I told you earlier?' and then excitedly shared their banter (which she was able to recall word for word).

Sameen: Have you ever been to the moon?
Simran: Of course I have. I go there every day.
Sameen: [Laughing] No one even takes you to the next town yet you've been to the moon.

Then, pausing for a few seconds, she added: Or maybe you could start with the thing about the painter. She asked me once, 'What would you think of a man wearing a suit and tie who was dancing on the street?' I said, 'An idiot'. She got so angry with me that she didn't speak to me for the next few days. Other writers tried to get us to stop our fight. They would call me and I would say, 'I don't want to talk to that crazy old woman', and she would say, 'I don't want to talk to that rude, egoistic girl'. It was such a small argument but we didn't talk to each other for weeks and then we had one last phone call that was two days before her death.

There are different vantage points for narrating this story. The bare facts are simple enough. Two writers liked each other's stories and became friends. They confided in and drew strength from each other. Their friendship continued for several years, but they never met each other. Then one of them unexpectedly passed away. These are the facts, but how does one evoke the vibrant colours of their friendship or the depth of their unconditional affection for each other? Simran's anecdotes about their conversations, the tone of her voice as she shared them, helped me sense this. Let us therefore proceed through these anecdotes, treating them as stepping-stones that might bring us closer to the sense of these friendships.

Their friendship began after Sameen read some of Simran's work and asked the editor for her phone number. They were both very different. Unlike Simran, Sameen had a strong sense of politics and felt deeply about issues such as the declining standards of literature in her regional language. She read digests but preferred to have her own fiction published in literary magazines. Personally, her life was relatively isolated. She lived with a sibling; there was little emotional connection, however, partly because of her decision to leave her husband. She lived in a separate portion of the house and was frequently alone. Sameen was a prolific writer, but there was no monetary compensation.

> She was so silly; she would even buy the literary magazines her own work had been published in because the editors would not send a complimentary copy. The money her family gave her for shoes or clothes, she would spend that on these things. Like one day she told me she had Rs 700 [$7] for shoes but she spent it on literary magazines.

Sameen had met a man she loved, but several complications made their union unlikely. 'He used to call her every Friday, so on that day I would begin by asking her about the hopeless lover [aashiq-e-na murad].' While Sameen hoped to marry this man, her daily moments were intertwined with Simran's presence.

> Should I tell you something funny [aik mazay ki baat bataoon]. I would tease Sameen so much. She would wake up around Tahajjud time [3 a.m.] and I would call her then. She would say 'This is my

time with Allah' and then I would say 'Just go back to sleep but keep the phone on, so I can hear your silence'. She would be so touched. 'This is how much you love me,' and you know what I would do then? [Laughing] I would turn on the radio and put the phone next to it; she would get so angry with me.

Simran, was also friends with one of Sameen's relatives who was also a writer. She did not, however, realise they were related till a few months later. Sameen shared little about her family but what went through her mind, thoughts she pondered and emotions she experienced, were all shared with Simran. They had exchanged pictures (one photograph each). Simran had saved it in her phone but lost it when it broke. 'I wish I had recorded her voice. Sameen had recorded mine once and then told me she listened to it every day. She used to call me her battery charger, because she would feel low when she didn't hear my voice.' After their argument about the painter, Simran didn't hear from Sameen for a few days, and then she received an unexpected call. 'She was still angry with me but when she heard me cough, she got concerned. "Simran, why are you coughing? Have you taken something for this?" She began telling me about her recent story about a man who is exhausted and searching for comfort. Then the divine gathers him in like a mother gently holds her tired child.'

In a sense, all that's left of Sameen now are stories. Not just the ones she wrote, but those about her. A published digest story depicts her as a woman who was hurt by the man she loved and was unable to bear the pain. An unpublished digest story provides a more accurate depiction of her life. Simran has sent it to the editor, but it is on hold as Simran considers whether the details are too identifiable. The depiction Simran treasures most is of their friendship. She was forced to write it when the editor of the literary magazine to which Sameen contributed asked her for a memorial. Simran thereupon sent in the pages she had written as she sought to cope with her grief. The piece is addressed to Sameen and weaves in their banter and affection. The editor later told Simran he had found himself crying as he read it and published it without any changes. Simran also sent it to a digest editor. in this case, the editor published it as a fictional account and changed the pronouns so it was framed as a man writing for a woman he'd lost. In this sense, just as Sameen's life has been painted in different colours, so has Simran's depiction of their relationship. It takes on different shades and evokes different reactions as it circulates. It moved one editor to tears and another to confusion and a subsequent correction of changing the context.

Once I overheard Simran's sister worriedly telling her, 'You've not eaten anything; at least have something now'. This, coupled with Simran's sleep disturbances I already knew about, prompted me to talk to a friend who provided grief counselling. Simran was still struggling with Sameen's loss, and I felt unsure about the degree to which it had affected her daily functioning. Another concern was that Simran would sometimes address me as Sameen, and I was not sure how to react to that without hurting her feelings. After the psychologist had asked me a few questions about Simran and Sameen, she seemed puzzled and said, 'I may be wrong, but my understanding of the bond between this person and the friend she has lost sounds like one between spouses.' I could understand her confusion but felt that if she had been a digest reader or writer, the emotional intimacy of voices would not have been so surprising.

CONVERSATIONS AS CONNECTIONS?

This chapter demonstrates how absence and anonymity lead to a certain emergence of presence and identity. Let us briefly turn again to Derrida (1967), who stated that oppositional concepts blend into one another; there is no airtight binary and therefore strict categories of experience actually interweave these concepts. Presence can bring absence, and absence can bring presence. For instance, the anonymity of Internet chat rooms or online exchanges often brings (to presence) inclinations of abuse and harassment that may be absent in everyday life, and therefore the prevalence of cat-fishing, child sexual exploitation, even simple verbal abuse and harassment that form an intrinsic part of today's online world. In this context, absence or a lack of identity markers makes it easier to venture into and explore avenues that militate against human ethics. However, this can also be positive, and this is what I have demonstrated in this chapter by tracing bonds that are predicated on sound and emerge in the absence of physical presence.

There is however also another way of exploring these conversations. One interesting vantage point is through the French philosopher Gilles Deleuze's concept of connections and unfolding actualisations. These terms are contextualised within the framework of the larger question for him: who we are and what we might become.

One of the central questions for anthropology is: what are the different ways in which people articulate their humanness? In other words, how do humans live? Philosophy approaches the same question but from its own district standpoint. For Deleuze, the larger question is how one might live.[19] This question is not, however, a prescription, nor does it assume only humans. For Deleuze, it can mean humans, relationships, body parts, movements, gestures, or eras; his point being that the correct way of understanding the world is not through the perspective of a human subject. The future is concerned with experimentation; we can discover our possibilities as a human but we can also discover the possibilities of relationships, conversations, individual body parts, movements, and eras (May, 2003: 150–70), or in our case, conversations and friendships.

How does this relate specifically to our discussion in this chapter? In the earlier paragraphs, I have highlighted an attunement to emotions where conversations unfold in unexpected ways. This unfolding can be unexpected, because the absence of the usual markers of identity creates a space where our position as subjects is destabilised in a certain sense. In speaking to these writers, I initially did position myself as an academic or a researcher but with the passage of time, the bonding was not rooted in any of the specific identities I held. Instead, it was rooted in emotions and the sharing of these emotions and the life experiences that led to them. In this context, the conversations assumed a life of their own. The conversations were not really conducted as such but entailed a stepping back. It is usually in speaking that we understand what we want to say, as the Austrian–British philosopher Ludwig Wittgenstein (1953) aptly observes. Thus, the absence of identity markers in speaking allowed certain forms of expression to emerge that would not otherwise have been the case. Usually, our identity defines the contours of our conversations and interaction with others but in these interactions, the conversation begins to unfold and allows for new avenues of identity. In other words, the conversation shapes our identity (both for us and the other) rather than the other way around.

This is similar to what the philosopher Todd May (2005) describes in the context of body parts and their interaction that goes beyond subject positions, as he explained Deleuze's philosophy. We all know what we should be attracted to based on our gender, sexual identities, and conventional notions of beauty. Yet our body parts also function at a pre-individual level. In other words, there is an unconscious connection that comes through but does not rely on particular individuals. The dichotomy of *I* and *you* becomes destabilised yet it does not lead to *us*, but rather to a certain web of sensations and objects (body parts) that both create and perceive those sensations.

> The hand that caresses the stomach is not telling anything to the stomach nor to the individual whose stomach it is. It is connecting to the stomach, exploring it. And in doing so is creating sensations that are not, strictly speaking, either mine or yours or ours. There

is no possession of the sensation, and there is no subject of it. If we want to put it in terms of individuals, we might say that each of us is the object of the sensation rather than its subject. But each of us is not the only object. The hand, the stomach: they are also the objects of sensation ... (particularly when love deepens). I do not caress your stomach. My hand caresses it. Automatically and without decision. There is always something outside our identification as subjects and persons (2005: 168).

How would visceral engagement, as described in the passage above, work here, as the larger context for us is that of disembodied voices? Let us turn to the literary theorist Karen Littau (2006). To reiterate, she argues that given the suspension of disbelief, we experience an 'incoherent I' through fiction reading as our usual solidity as an autonomous subject is dissolved. This is not always a simple case of identifying with the characters and feeling what they feel—but these affective delights can also be visceral in nature (2006: 74–6). The relationship of reader and text is also a bodily one, not just in the sense of our perception of a book's ideas being affected through its material form but also because reading entails a certain bodily engagement, even if we are only moving our eyes. As I elaborated in the 'Introduction', she draws on the history of reading to show how our current notion of reading as a cognitive, disembodied activity is a recent development. In our age, the concern about physiological reactions has shifted to television watching and social media. However, this shift in conventional understanding does not mean that the relationship between a reader and text is no longer one between two bodies (the body of the book and that of the reader).

In this context, it seems comparable to air travel, which initially led to involuntary bodily reactions such as vomiting, but is now usually without any severe bodily reactions as our (modern) bodies have adjusted to the sense of being airborne. Similarly, given Littau's evidence, reading too appears to have induced such reactions that are no longer prevalent but that does not mean that reading does not involve any visceral bodily engagement.

These connections entail an attunement to emotions but there is also a certain element of flow that is similar to what May describes through his example of the connection between the hand and the stomach. The conversation with Raheela that led to a blurring of my position as an academic and her position as a prolific writer, or the conversation that evoked a writer's sharing of her childhood and my sharing of my father's illness, were not really conducted but felt and sensed. Just as the stomach and the hand in the example both create and are the object of that sensation, similarly, the conversations were created by us but not really as stable subjects. The experience was not really one of acting but simultaneous acting and being acted upon. I did not consciously plan on sharing my experience of my father's illness; it happened, and, because my usual identity markers were not present, this happening allowed a certain emergence of feelings that remain in the background during my everyday interactions with other people. In this context, these conversations are an unfolding, a discovering or opening in which each of us is both the subject and object of the conversation. As Deleuze put it, 'This is how it should be done; lodge yourself on a stratum, experiment with the opportunities it offers, find an advantageous path on it, find potential movements of deterritorialisation'.[20]

At one level, every relationship is an actualisation of possibilities. There is always conscious effort involved in terms of who we choose to interact with, befriend, or spend our life with based on our values and ways of looking at the world. However, at another level, the element of chance, uncertainty, and unexpected encounters or new directions always exists. How many of us can explain growing close to one person rather than another solely as a rational, conscious decision? Chance, randomness—even factors such as spatiality— play a role. In other words, each relationship has a life of its own; it contains an element of our conscious choice and identity but there is also much else. In the context of the digest community, this 'much else' plays a more visible role, and one possible vantage point is the Deleuzian framework of unfolding actualisations.

Finally, let us return to emotional attunement as a norm of engagement in these conversations. During research, as we enter a different turf, we have to justify our intrusion by framing ourselves as someone who can be trusted with a relationship or even simple information. However, what I assumed to be a predicate of the writer's and reader's trust was often irrelevant to them.[21] Here, norms of engagement were different, and my own compass too needed to shift. The implicit norms of engagement in graduate seminars, such as linear logic and a perspective based on reason, are gradually (graduate-ly) ingrained as we strive for an academic identity. Here, however, these had to be unlearned as communication predicated on making sense was replaced by conversations focused on making one feel: important, loved, understood, held, and heard.

Notes

1. Verse by a South Asian Sufi saint, Bulleh Shah. *Bulleh Shah: A Selection*, trans. Taufiq Rafat, Oxford University Press, 2016.
2. Derrida elaborated his concept of deconstruction in his 1967 work entitled *Of Grammatology*. He positioned this exploration as following through on the German philosopher Heidegger's concern that, in focusing on clarity and distinctness, traditional philosophy had lost sight of the mystery and weight that any phenomenon carries.
3. Factors such as licensing for private channels, their need to fill airtime, and the initial success of televised plays based on digest narratives have created an expanding niche in the electronic media for digest writers. Thus, over the past decade, digest narratives that had previously circulated in print form have increasingly been adapted for visual media.
4. Interview with *Pakeeza*'s editor, Anjum Ansar, June 2012.
5. Telephonic interview, July 2012.
6. John Llewelyn (2012), 'David Wood's Reflections on the Lure of the Writer's Cabin: An Endorsement'.
7. An Internet search of her name presents a photo of a young woman; however, her Facebook page explains that this is not her and there are no public photos of her. After her wedding in 2014, two photographs of the

function were circulated on the Internet by someone, but this was followed by requests by her (posted on her Facebook page) to remove them.

8. Highlighted by Kara Wentworth in personal communication.

9. Also see Kathleen Stewart (2015), 'On Regionality', *The Geographical Review*, 103(2): 275–84.

10. I chose to keep the emoticons here to convey a sense of the tone embodied by these messages.

11. Text message from Kulsum (fictitious name), August 2012.

12. Telephonic interview, July 2012.

13. The anthropologist Brian Larkin observes that media products are not just objects people use; they also create certain sensory sensibilities relating to light, rhythm, and sound that are a part of an emotional experience of urban life. His primary question is to explore what is at stake in the encounter between subjects (Hausa) and new media technologies. In his work on Nigerian cinema, he suggests that media tools are not simply products that people use but form the sensory experience of urban life, 'an emotional experience based on a sensory environment regulated by specific relations of lighting, vision, movement, and sociality' (2008: 244, 319). A particularly interesting example is that of the aesthetic of outrage that Nigerian films employ (people not being what they seem; for instance, businessmen who join cults to increase their prospects of success). The experience of outrage by the audience is not just cognitive but a viscerally felt, collective reaction that is an intrinsic part of the sensory experience of cinema.

14. The sectarian killing of 45 Ismailis (a minority sect) was carried out by students of an elite business school, which led to questions about indoctrination by extremist religious parties on campuses around Pakistan.

15. The editor explained her decision as fearing a backlash by religious parties which were protesting against the army.

16. Anjum Ansar, 'Editorial', *Pakeeza*, January 2015.

17. My permanent employment at a local university entailed this emotional investment, as this was where I was going to be living and raising my children after receiving my PhD.

18. Once, when I was ill, she sent me a text suggesting that we make a deal with the divine. The bargain had to do with her falling ill instead of me. Historically, the Mughal Emperor Babar is supposed to have prayed to the divine to afflict him with the illness afflicting his son. There are different versions of this, but a popular one is that he circled his dying son's bed seven times, and from that day, he began to fall ill while his son's health progressively improved.

19. In ancient philosophy this question was framed as how we should live, the underlying assumption being that the cosmos is a larger whole, of which

individual lives are a part. Thus, human lives were seen as part of a larger cosmological order, and each philosopher's notions of what this cosmological order was varied. This later changed as the underlying assumption of conforming to a unified cosmos was replaced with individualism, a life being judged on its own merits based on universal moral codes and a transcendent order represented by God. With continental philosophy, in particular of Nietzsche, another question arose. Nietzsche's proclamation of the death of God was framed in the context of how one might act if there were no transcendent order (represented by God) or universal moral code. In other words, if there is no transcendence that diminishes or sustains us, then how do we articulate who we are and what we can become? Subsequently, Derrida, Foucault, and Sartre all adopted this Nietzschean assumption and provided different answers. Sartre perhaps framed it best: 'If God does not exist, we find no values or commands to turn to which legitimise our conduct. So, in the bright realm of values, we have no excuse behind us, nor justification before us. We are alone with no excuses' (*Existentialism*: 23). As all three (Derrida, Foucault, and Sartre) pointed out, we can evade addressing this question. This is because there is an intrinsic link between how we see ourselves and our worlds and the ways in which we live our lives. Foucault pointed out that there are particular ways of seeing the world, but these are not 'insurpassable', or inescapable because they arise from 'temporary historical circumstances rather than anthropological constraints' (May, 2005: 150–68).

20. Deleuze quoted in May (2005: 25).

21. For instance, one evening as a writer asked me about details of my work, I began to frame it in the context of anthropology. I could sense her attention drifting, and she stopped me midway, explaining that she only needed to know to be able to her to tell her admin (volunteers who manage her Facebook page) because they had asked about this. In contrast, the fact that I'd been a digest reader since seventh or eighth grade evoked both her trust and tenderness.

2

In Quest of Stories: Writers, Readers, and Fiction

The first chapter presented an ethnographic account of interacting with readers and writers, and highlighted how friendships are formed in physical absence. This chapter continues that trajectory by showing how the dynamic of bonds formed in physical absence is depicted in digest stories. It shares two digest stories and traces how digest writers depict lived realities, both of attachments in the digest community and the larger dynamics of living as a woman in Pakistan. Specifically, I begin by sharing a digest story to demonstrate how writers portray the dynamic of physical absence in their bonds with each other. I highlight the theme of absence and emotional intensity depicted in the story and suggest that although this emotional intensity is common in the friendships between readers and writers, it exists in tandem with, rather than in contrast to, mainstream notions of heterosexual desire. In this context, I draw on the literary theorist Sharon Marcus (2007), who discusses forms of intense engagement between women. The second half of the chapter changes scale to demonstrate how these fictional stories articulate imagined possibilties and lived experiences of being a woman in Pakistan. I draw on two specific theoretical frameworks: the literary scholar Judith Butler (1990), who posits the question of being a woman as open and ongoing, and feminist scholars Tharu and Lalitha (1993), who identify South Asian women's journals in the nineteenth and early twentieth centuries as a site where questions such as child marriage and women's education were being negotiated by women. Drawing on these frameworks, I proceed to show how personal desires, lived moments in Pakistan's history, and notions of how a woman should behave texture these narratives by tracing the specific form these take in a writer's work. I then share a digest story that depicts themes such as women's work empowerment and familial conflict. I contextualise the story by connecting it to specific realities of women's paid employment in Pakistan and then share my own engagement with the same story as a digest reader.

This chapter explores digest fiction as a site where various vantage points regarding the fluid, lived reality of being a Pakistani middle-class woman are articulated. Desires and conflicts are made public through a fictional form that allows them to remain private. It follows two specific insights of a politics of stance: (a) the move beyond a quick funnelling of digest narratives into progressive/retrogressive; and (b) positioning these fictional accounts as specifically embedded in social practices at particular moments in Pakistan (Ali, 2004). Within this framework, the chapter examines questions such as: How do digest writers depict bonds of friendship formed in the absence of physical proximity? How can these friendships be contextualised within the larger framework of homosocial bonds between women? How are lived realities such as women's entry into the workforce and familial dynamics articulated in digest fiction? How do individual readers appropriate stories within the context of their everyday lives and personal circumstances?

'SHADOWS OF IMAGINATION': A DIGEST STORY

Let us begin by exploring a digest story which presents the theme of friendships formed in the absence of physical proximity. The story revolves around two friends, Uneeza and Seema. Written in first person, it begins with Seema relating to us her fearful state of mind.

She is temporarily living in her old family home as a break from teaching responsibilities. However, instead of finding the peace she hoped for through this solitude, she feels alone and uneasy. As she shares her anxiety with us, there is a persistent knocking on the door. It adds to her jitteriness, and she imagines the presence of otherworldly ghosts and spirits.

Bad spirits? Noori began to laugh. 'Oh no, Bibi, it's only the poor postman. He had earlier brought a registered letter for you. You were not here; his home is nearby, maybe he's—the bell is ringing again.'

'Oh, my God,' I tried to force myself to laugh. 'Okay, bring it in.' A few minutes later, I had the letter in my hand. I kept thinking who could send a letter here for me. Fearfully, I opened it, but as soon as I looked at the handwriting, I kissed it with joy. I was so lost in it that I forgot that the environment was terrifying [haibathnaak]. I became so engrossed in the letter that I became oblivious to everything around me.

'The Life of my world [jaan-e-jahaan], Seemi, accept my love [pyaar lo]. You must be surprised at how your Uneeza suddenly remembered you after four years. You are so disloyal [baywafa]; in these four years you never even thought of writing to me once.'

Seema introduces Uneeza as a friend 'whose body is separate, but who shares the same soul [rooh]'. This is followed by a passage about how she does not even feel the sensation of time as she excitedly writes back to her friend.

Uneeza receives Seema's answer and we are privy to the letter again.

My darling [pyaree], lots of love [mohabbatein], I was about to die from happiness. After such a tough waiting period, I have my dear Seema's lovely, lovely writing. If you ask me, your letter blessed me with treasures of happiness. I picked up my Seema's letter, touched it to my eyes, and kissed it.

Through her letter, Uneeza tells Seema of having met a man named Aiman, whom she's soon going to marry. Her joy is obvious, but Seema shares with the readers that she has begun to feel envious of her friend's new-found familial bliss.

Her days have changed so drastically, and here I am with nothing. There is only my heart, and that too is riddled with desire [paamal-e-arzoo]. This time, my reply didn't have that enthusiasm or the warmth of sincerity or the restlessness of love. This spring, she and Aiman (the man she loves) will be one; why would she need me? This feeling hurts me.

A few months pass by, and there's another letter from Uneeza.

Seema, I am going crazy these days. Something has made me very restless [baytaab]. The necessity of being apart [doori ki majboori] tortures me. A week ago, Aiman went to the city to get some stuff for our wedding—he hasn't returned yet. My heart is not in anything; nothing holds any attraction. These days and night sting me.

Uneeza gets married, and Seema sends gifts for her wedding.

Days pass by. One day, I received the joyful news that she had become a mother. Even at this time, she could not forget me. She had written to me from the hospital and sent the photograph of her little baby. I quietly congratulated Seema's beautiful image in my mind. Lost in the whirlwind of memories, I suddenly noticed the stamp marks on the letter. Uneeza had written that she was in the hospital, but the stamps were the same as they always were. A few days later, she wrote to thank me for the toys I had sent for the baby. Now our correspondence was just a formality [rasmi ho gai thi]. That sincerity and that restlessness due to delayed letters were no longer there. She was a homemaker [gharast aurat]; she didn't have time anymore. But still, to some extent I was grateful that she remembered me and wrote to me.

'Seema, forgive me. I couldn't approach you earlier. I am very
worried these days. First, Aiman became very ill, so ill that it was
as if he turned back from God's abode. Now the little one is ill. I
don't understand his illness. I don't know what has happened. Every
day the doctor comes, and the prescription is changed, but, tell me,
Seema, will my baby never get well; will he never laugh again? Tell
me, Seema, that it will not be so.'

My heart brimmed with grief. I couldn't feel peace. I wrote several
letters to inquire about the baby's health, and I sent many telegrams,
but there was no reply. I held myself back for hardly a month and
a half or so. It wasn't with patience—I spent those days waiting on
hot coals. The eternal separation of that baby would pierce my heart
with arrows. I hoped it wouldn't happen, and before thinking any
further, I left for her house.

Seema arrives at the railway station and asks a taxi driver to take
her to the given address.

I asked a man standing nearby if he knew where Ashiana was. He
touched his ears with his hands [a gesture of asking forgiveness
from God] and said, 'Ya Allah tauba. What kind of names have
people started keeping now? God save us; is the time of Stone Age
coming back again, when humans lived like monkeys?'

After wandering fruitlessly for a while, the taxi driver asks her if
she knows of any other relatives, as no one seems to know Aiman.
Seema instead begins to ask people for Uneeza.

A few minutes later, my taxi was standing in front of a dilapidated
house. I was looking around in shock. Is that Ashiana, the beautiful
blue house? Surrounded by green trees? Fountains? Car? Garden?
I was so taken aback that I couldn't even walk. The taxi driver
knocked on the door.

As Seema finally enters the house, she sees Uneeza.

Soiled clothes, unkempt hair, terrifying eyes. I was shaken [*main laraz gai*]. She looked at me but didn't display any enthusiasm and turned her face. 'Uneeza'—I went ahead and hugged her—'come to your senses! What have you done to yourself? For God's sake, take care of your heart [*dil ko sambhalo*]. For my sake.'

Seema sees a man with 'helplessness in his eyes'. Uneeza calls him Aiman, but he tells Seema that he is Dr Joseph and is here to take Uneeza to the mental hospital.

Your friend is very emotional. In her imagination she would create homes surrounded by green trees and huge palaces. She naturally filled these spaces with her husband and baby. I was her doctor. I tried to stop her before she might go so far in her imagination that turning back would become impossible. But my poor child, she would laugh at this suggestion. She would say, 'Doctor, this world has not given me anything, but my imagination gives me peace. These walls, these creepy [*makrooh*] ceilings, these cobwebs—they entangle me. It is not possible to escape from them. I can't even go out of this cage. Let me be lost in the world where my husband is, where my baby exists.'

As the doctor explains the 'collision of her real world and imaginary world', Uneeza glances at Seema.

I screamed and ran. The cab was waiting for me. I fell inside, and I could only utter one word: 'Run!' [*bhaago*] The taxi sped ahead. I saw the deserted paths [*sunsaan veeranay*] of the afternoon, where terrifying whirlwinds [*bagoolay*] were rising. I rested my head on the seat. These whirlwinds are so horrifying. They arise in our minds [*insaanon ke dimagh main*] and take away our lives, consume them, and remove them from the plane of existence, leaving us nothing but destruction [*uski zindagi ko apnay andar samait kar safah-e-dehr se humesha ke liye nist o nabood kar daitay hain*].[1]

Let's first explore the absence of physical proximity and how its subsequent presence leads to the destruction of the relationship as well as the fictional world built through letters.

Seema and Uneeza are central to each other's lives. Seema's family is non-existent, whereas Uneeza's exists through her relationship with Seema. Her husband and baby assume meaning and become real for her as she shares that world with Seema. In other words, the ebb and flow of excitement, concerns, and fears for her family are shared through letters, and this sharing makes them emotionally real for Uneeza. The letters in this sense become a lifeline for her imaginary family. However, as Seema withdraws, the baby and husband fade away, leading Uneeza to repeatedly question Seema whether the baby would 'live'.

Uneeza desires a beautiful home, loving husband, and a child, as romance genres prescribe. However, her desire for emotional connection with Seema supersedes subscribed notions of desire. Seema's desires revolve around the same triad, and she is envious of Uneeza. This is however accompanied by a sense of becoming insignificant, of no longer being the central figure in Uneeza's life. It becomes apparent when she asks 'Why would she think of me now (*ab voh kahan mujhay yaad karay gi*)? The whirlwinds (*bagoolay*) in the last paragraph can therefore be both Seema's and Uneeza's. Uneeza's mental breakdown is explained to us (through the doctor) as a 'collision of her real world and imaginary world', but the imaginary world is not just Seema's. Uneeza relates to it too, and her fears of insignificance are an important, if not the primary, factor in destroying it.

There is also a very interesting dynamic regarding risks of physical proximity. There is no mention of Seema being invited to Uneeza's wedding. The friendship is long-distance, and it continues as long as this physical distance is respected. Once those boundaries are overstepped, the 'beautiful home surrounded by trees' changes to 'piles of trash'. There is an implicit understanding that the friendship is anchored in emotional connection. This emotional connection is woven through suspended disbelief and thrives through interiority. Uneeza's family exists in her inner world; no one in her physical world can relate to them. It is impossible for Uneeza's maid and Dr Joseph to suspend their disbelief and experience her inner world because they share her outer world through physical proximity. However, Seema, because of her physical absence, can share and relate to the characters Uneeza forms. It is also interesting that nowhere in the story is there an overt desire to be with each other in person. Seema goes over to Uneeza's house because she is driven by fears about Uneeza's silence rather than a wish for physical proximity.

Aside from these two friends, there are five marginal characters. The only two other women are Uneeza's and Seema's maids. In some sense they act as gateways between the inner and outer. The story begins as Seema shares her anxiety. As readers, we listen to her fears but we are unable to assuage or change them because we only know the world through her. Her maid, Noori, connects the outer world to the inner. The postman remains in the background, an unknown that is translated by Noori and transformed from a frightening 'persistent knock' to the ordinariness of a postman at the door.

As Seema enters her friend's house, Seema's maid opens the door and takes her to Uneeza, completing the circle that began with Noori, who handed her the letter. Thus, in both cases, women who share physical proximity mark the beginning and end of the imaginary world created by Seema and Uneeza.

Aside from Aiman, who remains invisible, we have Dr Joseph, an unnamed, middle-aged man whom Seema encounters, and the taxi driver.

The poetic Ashiana to which Seema asks for directions evokes the unnamed man's disapproval. This disapproval is couched in the language of religiosity which often accompanies critiques of digest writing. The other man, Dr Joseph, is introduced through his 'helpless expressions'. He is sympathetic, but he too disapproves of

Uneeza's flights into her imaginary world. Therefore, at one level, we can see these two characters as representing the disapproval digest writers have to face in their real lives. The middle-aged man represents the common stereotype of digest writers and readers as frivolous women who waste time on meaningless stories rather than engaging with meaningful religious books. Dr Joseph represents the English-speaking public which encourages rationality and views digest writing as an escape, a sort of slipping away rather than stoically facing up to what life has to offer. I also find it significant that Seema's encounter with the middle-aged man does not topple their shared world. Digest writers often create stories in a sort of inverted image of their everyday lives. The everyday disappointments of neglectful husbands and financial problems are eased when they are replaced with attentive, caring spouses and financial security. Therefore disappointments lead to desires, which in turn inform their imagination. For instance, a judgemental spouse or parent often leads to the fictional creation of a supportive one. Seema easily ignores the judgemental attitude of the middle-aged man. However, Dr Joseph, the rational healer who is concerned by Uneeza's flights of imagination, proves to be more challenging. Uneeza has tried to change him into Aiman, but he refuses that and eventually gets her locked up.

Let us now turn to the taxi driver. We could look at him as subscribed notions of desire which are publicly accepted. We inhabit both (taxis as well as desires) for their promise of taking us elsewhere. We ride in them, expecting to be taken to a destination. In other words, socially constructed notions of desires such as familial bliss hold a promise. The promise is one of closure, fulfilment, or anchoring: the feel of reaching a destination. What that fulfilment will feel like, or what it means to us, is personal in each case. Motivations for inhabiting are private and personal. These are, however, also public and socially constructed notions; the taxi driver steers the vehicle for us.

The inner and the outer begin colliding for Seema the moment she begins interacting with the taxi driver. For brevity, I do not share certain sections of the story which contains several paragraphs describing Seema's annoyance with the taxi driver who doubts the existence of the blue house which she wants to reach. While Noori (the maid) is a source of emotional comfort, the taxi driver's presence adds to her emotional exhaustion. Towards the end, however, she leaves the situation in the same taxi which is waiting for her. The literal vehicle becomes a metaphorical one too, and she runs away from the turmoil of her and Uneeza's shared world by inhabiting the taxi of publicly acceptable desires.

Pushing this a little further, the taxi could also be seen as the romance genre. We are essentially fragmented beings with fragmented desires. As Oliver Sacks (2010) argued, even the basic sense of sight is essentially a 'soup of visual sensations' which is plotted and put into recognisable boxes such as 'cat' or 'table'. This happens at an unconscious level, but the truth of this process is borne out by experiences of people who suddenly gain the sense of sight. 'I see a cat,' for them, is preceded by, 'I see a tail, four legs, and fur', and it takes perceptional filtering to put that together into a cat.[2]

My point in sharing this example is that even simple visual perception requires a centring, a kind of putting together of the relevant and filtering out of the irrelevant. The world is constructed rather than given. Desires, too, are fragmented and require a similar framing and centring. The romance genre functions as a key site where desires are made comprehensible, given a certain direction through notions of family, married couple, love, and sexuality. The literary theorist Lauren Berlant aptly identifies this role as she points out:

> As sites for theorising and imaging desire, they manage
> ambivalence, designate the individual as the unit of social
> transformation; reduce the overwhelming world to an intensified

space of personal relations; establish dramas of love, sexuality, and reproduction as the dramas central to living; and install the institutions of intimacy (most explicitly the married couple and the intergenerational family) as the proper sites for providing in which a subject has a 'life' and a 'future' (Berlant, 2012: 95).

At one level then, we enter the world of romance fiction to experience a simpler, more comprehensible world, where fulfilment is clearly charted out through orbits of interpersonal relations, family, and marriage. A part of us is aware that both our inner and outer world of interpersonal relations is far more complicated. However, during the time of suspended disbelief of reading romance fiction, we are able to relinquish that heavy complexity. Returning to the taxi analogy, reading fiction becomes a taxi ride, where we cease to navigate and are driven elsewhere. The decision to ride in a taxi or read a romance story is our own, but the navigation is not. In other words, finding a way to 'elsewhere' is temporarily abdicated in both. How does this connect to the story under discussion and the bonds of trust we are exploring? Seema leaves the complexity of her relationship with Uneeza by running away in a taxi. In this context, the taxi as a metaphor for digest genre works at two levels. First, it becomes a stabilising factor, balancing the overwhelming emotions she feels for Uneeza. Second, it helps her navigate her way back to safety. This could entail mainstream notions of normality, or perhaps notions of desire, but in either case, it's an 'elsewhere'.

BONDS BETWEEN WOMEN

To explore how this story relates to the bonds of trust between digest readers and writers, let us again briefly turn to the relationship between Seema and Uneeza. As mentioned in the earlier paragraphs, they are both central to each other's lives. This centrality is expressed and contoured through terms of endearment usually reserved for lovers. Uneeza addresses Seema as 'life of my world' and 'my love', and Seema tells us about Uneeza as someone whose body is separate but who shares her soul. They kiss each other's letters, touch them to their eyes, and openly express intense attachment to each other. These expressions are not uncommon in the bonds between readers and writers. The bonds of trust are intense, and affection is openly expressed through similar phrases.[3]

Yet there is the simultaneous dynamic of the centrality of marriage and heterosexual romance. Conversations are peppered with anecdotes about husbands, fiancés, or desires for a fulfilling marriage. This is not compensation as such, highlighting a socially acceptable desire to balance an 'unacceptable' one. Rather, desires revolve around heterosexual relationships and coexist with attachments between women.

Attachments between women can be viewed as a kind of playful, innocuous flirtation that is managed and stabilised because of the common subscription to conventionality. Being a regular reader or writer of digest fiction reflects your implicit endorsement of conventional notions of marriage and family. Homosexuality is present in the digest discourse but as something that is to be avoided. This is stated in direct editorial responses as well as certain subtle stories. For instance, an editorial response to a letter sent under 'psychological problems' forbids a reader from same-sex desire in the following words:

> To love someone of your own gender is sexual deviance, and with great sorrow I have to say that you are a victim of this deviance. Love has degrees; the love for a husband cannot be given to a girl. The path you are on is one of destruction. Before you fall into this pit, pull yourself together and ask for forgiveness from Allah.[4]

Homosexuality is thus articulated as deviance, but intensity and 'romance-like' interaction between women is both openly accepted and depicted. Numerous stories published around the same time as the previous editorial prohibition portray this intensity.

The thought of her superseded everything in my mind. Each time I
would sit down to read a book, I would see her face on every page.
Picking up the newspaper, I would see her reflection in every line;
she would be on the calendar pictures too. I would get annoyed
and turn the page, but she would still be present. I tore up many
calendars in this state of mind. I was stuck in the vortex of thoughts
about her.[5]

> We were both friends. I don't know if she loved me, but I loved
her immensely ... she resided in the palace of my heart ... I had
made her a part of not just my heart but also my soul.[6]

How do readers and writers reconcile this apparent tension of
a sexual nature? It is usually addressed through the concept of
spiritual romance *(roohani* romance). Actual romance is seen as
being oriented toward men and mainstream notions of family and
marriage. However, emotional fulfilment is also found through
deep affection between women, and this is 'spiritual romance'
which does not violate any boundaries so long as it is expressed
and felt through words. It is because readers and writers implicitly
subscribe to traditional conceptions of marriage and family that
this playfulness and intensity can be easily explored and indulged
in. The effusive, romantic phrases in text messages and letters
are viewed as spiritual so long as they remain on this level. Their
intrusion into the domain of heterosexual marriage or family is
viewed as a transgression.

SAME-SEX DESIRE

Taking into account the earlier discussion, fiction as the 'space
for desire' provides a law and a structure where one re-encounters
oneself in stories about who an individual is and what they want:
'stories to which one clings so as to be able to reencounter oneself
as solid and in proximity to being idealisable' (Berlant, 2012: 76). It
provides a space but also a 'law for desire' that is as contradictory
as any other law. In a sense, it centres desire around mainstream

notions of family and male validation, yet it also carries dynamics or flows where the social bonds between women de-centre mainstream notions of desire. Therefore, in the digest genre, desire in the narrow sense of the word, between men and women, is occasionally pushed into the background by desire in the broader sense of the term of homosocial bonds between women.

The dynamics shared previously are not exceptional or specific to the digest genre. Other mainstream romance genres also contain similar depictions of female dyads. For instance, a popular Pakistani movie, *Saheli* (female friend), carries the same motifs of sacrifice, deep affection, and nurturing bonds as the digest story shared earlier.[7] Exploring the theme of polygamy depicted in the movie (the two women live with each other when they decide to get married to the same man), Kamran Ali (2014) asserts that although the two women protagonists were a part of the male-dominated society, the viewers also witness the bond between these two women as actually stronger than those they have with their respective male companions.[8] Thus, in this context, polygamy can be read as a cultural metaphor, a bowing to convention that lets the two individuals who want to be with each other live together through this institution. Therefore, through all the subplots and turns in the story, the ultimate union is between the two women. This is particularly poignant in the last scene when the camera focuses only on them and the husband remains off camera.

Ali's reading, shared in the previous paragraphs, helps us understand attachments amongst the digest public as it highlights the significance of homosocial relationships without funnelling it through the heterosexual and homosexual dichotomy. He draws on the literary theorist Sharon Marcus (2007), who highlights the importance of women's friendships in the Victorian era through her investigation of women's life writing. One of her central arguments is that middle-class women's attachments were intertwined in ways that go beyond the binary of homosexuality and heterosexuality. Men remained central in women's lives but this did not preclude the complex and strong bonds between women. There was thus no contest between homosexual and heterosexual desire. Attachments between women existed alongside heterosexual desire. Rather than a threat, they were socially acceptable and viewed as being morally uplifting. This is partly because, in contrast to emerging market forces and notions of competitiveness and instrumentality, these attachments were free of material entanglements and not seen as a means to any end. In a sense they were akin to a luxury good free from instrumentality; thus, having a friend meant a woman could afford to lavish time and attention on someone who did not in any way directly promote her interests. They focused on pure sentiment and were framed through gestures reflecting generosity, altruism, and mutual indebtedness.

Marcus's study is compelling, with myriad insights; however, we focus on four key aspects of her study that are directly parallel to the dynamics of the digest public.

First, these friendships allowed women to go beyond limits assigned to their gender without appearing mannish. They could adopt an active attitude toward the objects of their affection, a prerogative that is otherwise associated with men. Second, these friendships entailed playful behaviour and a space where women could be spontaneous in contrast to their more guarded relationships with men. Third, in contrast to the practical entanglements of family and marriage, where a person is born into a set of affinities, these relationships could be chosen. They allowed women to move closer to those with whom they connected, to make the first move, and to solidify amity through a variety of gestures. Finally, women who expressed these deep feelings for their women friends rarely met them. There was no physical proximity because they rarely saw each other in person.

The first three points help us understand why women in the digest public gravitate toward one another, and the last helps in understanding how these relationships work in tandem with rather than in contrast to mainstream notions of romance and family. Marcus (2007) emphasises that these relationships cannot be positioned as a form of pre-marriage practice because they continued long after the women married. The institution of marriage did not reduce the affection shared by women. They cannot be funnelled as sexual tension between women either, as there was no contest between heterosexual and homosexual desire. In other words, the texture of these friendships defies both under-interpretation as a stage to be overcome and over-interpretation as sexual acts.

> The annals of Victorian women's life-writing point again and again to female friendship's location at the heart of the hallowed middle-class institutions of marriage and family. Female friendship was a very different social bond from female marriage, though both enjoyed degrees of social acknowledgement and approval. It was also distinct from the unrequited loves and infatuations that were rarely disclosed beyond a very restricted private circle. Friendship allowed women to compete for and charm each other, to develop their intellectual and aesthetic tastes, to augment their worldly ties, and to deepen their spiritual ones. Its pleasures and passions were also closely allied to the love of kin and the delights of marriage. (Marcus, 2007: 72)

Marcus highlights that gradually, this began to change, and by the 1930s, it had lost its authenticity and was perceived simply as a stage to be overcome. It is interesting that a similar shift in perception can also be discerned in the digest genre. Based on a random sample of digests published from 1973 through 2015, I found that the stories depicting these intense friendships between women gradually disappear after the 1970s. The stories I have quoted are all from the 1970s, and the movie too is from 1960. However, although it has disappeared from mainstream media over the years, it may still exist in the relationships between women in the digest community.

Let us now change scale and turn to the second key question for this chapter: How are the contemporary realities of being a woman in Pakistan articulated in digest narratives, and how do individual readers appropriate certain stories within the context of their personal lives?

To Be a Woman?

In positing what it means to be a woman as an open and ongoing question, I draw on the feminist scholar Judith Butler (1990).[9] Butler (in a now familiar and much-cited argument) problematises the biological 'givenness' of being a woman or a man as she frames sex (or the binary of bodies into male and female) as culturally constructed and part of the gender system.[10] She suggests that sex is assigned rather than assumed and there are a variety of ways in which it can work. Thus, the binary of sex into male and female is a part of the gender system rather than something essential or natural. This is a particularly relevant observation for us because it allows us to examine how gendered categories come to be and how their meaning changes over time. Whereas Butler emphasises the 'performativity' of gender, the anthropologist Evelyn Blackwood (2006) focuses on the difference between dominant ideologies of gender and the spaces or gaps for disrupting these notions. She delineates between gender as a subjective experience and as a cultural category, and suggests that it comprises of two overlapping processes: a cultural category and a subjective experience. The study of gender as a cultural category enables us to identify how certain representations of masculinity or femininity are privileged and legitimised through dominant ideological discourses at the local and state level. Viewing gender as a subjective experience enables us to explore the processes of negotiation, displacement, and resistance that go into framing our identity as a subset of possible social identities. Therefore, gendered identities are a way for individuals to make sense of who they are, and these identities are embedded within structures that 'claim constancy and immutability' (Blackwood, 2006: 214).[11] Yet within these very structures there are gaps and spaces that allow for dissent. This is relevant for us because digest fiction is a site where dominant ideologies of gender (conventional understandings of beauty, roles of men and women) are reinforced. However, at the same time, there are gaps for dissent and alternative articulations. In other words, digest fiction is a site where dominant ideologies of what it means to be a Pakistani woman are reinforced, but the same site also contains gaps for negotiation and reworking.

South Asian women's journals as a primary site for dominant notions of both womanhood and its reworking is not a new phenomenon. Tharu and Lalitha (1993) identify popular journals for women as a crucial site where notions such as purdah, education, and child marriage were being negotiated and reworked during the colonial period. They suggest that women's texts from the nineteenth and early twentieth centuries are best read as documents which demonstrate writers' engagements with the reworking of the world that was formed through the colonial empire. Moreover, they position later texts (written in the twentieth century) as a re-articulation of the norms that were framed during the 1940s–50s and continue to underwrite culture and politics until the 1990s (Tharu and Lalitha, 1993: 43). Similarly, Talwar (1989) traces some of the more influential women's magazines and presents stories to demonstrate the principal frameworks of how questions regarding education and veiling were renegotiated through these writings. For instance, she points out that women had identified the lack of education as a primary obstacle (along with purdah and child marriage on the grounds that they prevented women's education). Nationalist leaders supported this demand for education but differed in terms of what kind of education was relevant for women (for example, indigenous or Western, academic or practical). In this context, women's journals of the time became a site where these demands were articulated both through fiction and non-fiction articles.

Digest writers come from various socioeconomic backgrounds and engage with the question of what it means to be a woman from a discursive standpoint. In this context, they can be posited as 'cultural citizens'. This is a term the anthropologist Rudolph Gaudio (2009), among others, uses to highlight that, along with citizenship within the state, there is a fluid framework of cultural citizenship. Our identities are embedded in social fields and institutions; thus, participation in social worlds means navigating on the basis of particular aesthetics, emotions, and beliefs, not just power relations. This is relevant here because writers consciously examine and articulate their negotiation with the prevalent cultural norms of femininity. This discursive engagement is through particular aesthetics, beliefs, and emotions about being a woman which are confirmed or contested by other digest writers or readers.

The social perception of these digests is generally that of frivolous fiction which panders to a demand for easy reading.[12] However, through ethnographic work, I realised that writers themselves see their role as one of imparting correct values that are necessary for an ethical Pakistani woman. Thus, they see themselves not as entertainers but educators whose task is to guide women, particularly young girls, in navigating Pakistan's changing social milieu. This perception is not a new development but has existed since the very inception of this genre as it emerged through the reformist movement of educating Muslim women. In the late nineteenth century, Muslim reformers resisted colonial influence by emphasising Muslim culture and Islamic laws as opposed to the realm of custom (deemed to be superstitious, un-Islamic, and irrational). This, in turn, led to an increased interest in educating Muslim women and the first specialised periodicals for women on the subcontinent (Ali, 2004: 125–6).

However, this process is accompanied with a validity of felt experiences. In their interactions with me, most digest writers stated that they wanted to write because some of the stories they were reading did not really reflect the life they experienced, and therefore wanted to 'correct it'. This was not really in terms of factual correction but rather an experiential, emotional one. Thus, the motivation to write was driven by a certain confidence in the validity of their felt experiences. In this way, by first reading and then writing, they become part of a 'particular kind of affective world' which authenticates, validates, and sometimes also potentially changes how they feel about their lives. Even after authors become well known, it's rare for family members, especially male family members (husbands or sons), to read their stories. Of all the writers I interviewed, only one said that her husband had read her work, and that too only the first one (because they had a bet on how much of it would be edited out). In this sense, then, what writers share of themselves through their stories, in this public genre, is actually quite private—not in the sense of sharing facts about their lives but shared feelings about lived experiences and imagined possibilities that are in the context of particular moments in time in Pakistan. This is similar to what Tharu and Lalitha (1993) identify in women's writings from the nineteenth and early twentieth centuries as women's reworking of the world around them.

Writers' Articulations of Imagined Possibilities and Lived Experiences

Let me now trace how personal desires, motivations, and public moments in Pakistan's political history intertwine by sharing a short bio of a writer and her novel. The writer, Rubab (fictitious name), heads a girls' college, and was very active in the leftist student union during her university days in the late 1970s. Her time at Punjab University overlapped Zulfiqar Ali Bhutto's elected government and the beginning of the 11-year period of martial law imposed by General Zia ul-Haq (1977–88). There were widespread protests against the imposition of martial law, particularly in universities. In consequence, often professors or protesting students were held in forced detention. Rubab's depiction of daily student life entails the initial effect of new rules, such as gender-segregated pathways, as well as the strange dynamics as government officials who were previously students at the university had to arrest and detain professors under whom they had studied.[13]

Rubab maintained a personal journal at the time and now weaves specific incidents from it into her serialised novel. Thus, her writing highlights a 'small voice in history' as she represents a turbulent historical time period in Pakistan through the specificity of a young woman's university life. Sitting on a sofa in her drawing room (the room reserved for guests), with the tape-recorder between us, she told me how she felt compelled to write as stories came to her. This sense of compulsion was not really in terms of telling the story of her own life, but more particularly in terms of an affective engagement (or entanglement) with the political turmoil around her and how that often manifested itself in certain images, real or imaginary, that she felt compelled to write about. She gave the example of her short story *Dastak* (Knock), about a political prisoner who gets shot and dies holding the flower a girl had earlier given to him. 'I was feeding my toddler and, Kiran, it was almost like this story suddenly jingled and landed inside me [*chunn se aik kahani meray andar aa utri*]. The image was so clear, like I had seen a film, but I hadn't.'[14]

Rubab didn't mention this, but other writers told me of her daughter's sudden death, which led to a 15-year hiatus in her writing. Abeer, the young woman whose life her current novel revolves around, is the same age as her daughter would have been had she survived. Moreover, during the interview, when I asked her which character she related to the most, rather than saying Abeer, as I expected her to, she spoke about Abeer's mother. In this context, her writing is not only about a moment in Pakistan's history but also her own desires in relation to the kind of woman she had wanted herself or her daughter to be. In her interview, Rubab stated how her writing was about Pakistan and the various phases through which it had passed. However, the characters she constructs to tell her stories (young women such as Abeer) and the sites she chooses to have them published (digests rather than a literary magazine) not only bring in a strong element of her own notions of what it means to be a woman in Pakistan but also open them up to a discursive engagement.

This is similar to what the anthropologist Caroline Humphrey identifies in her work on Russian memoirs and fiction. She suggests that communal buildings had meanings and effects which were at once specific to them and at the same time refracted outward. These can be seen as rays shot off a crystal; they could divert the ideological functionality of these buildings into 'vast or tiny longingful projections' (2005: 43). Such personal ruminations are social in that they are directed towards interpreting readers (a personal consciousness or that of others) who are also subjects of the universally distributed ideology. So such stories are social in that they are directed not just to a personal consciousness but also other subjects who are shaped by the same structures of ideology, power, desire, and aesthetics.

During the interview I found myself telling her of an earlier encounter. I had gone to a shrine named Bari Imam near my home town, the federal capital, Islamabad. I sat in the corner as women and children trailed in and out of the large domed structure. It was a relatively quiet day, and I found myself alone with another group who were wearing abayas. As I walked over toward the area where you could see the actual grave, one of them sternly addressed me and said, 'Your hair is showing; you need to cover it'. I had my head already covered, but with a loose dupatta rather than a tight hijab. To me that sufficed in terms of showing respect, but to her it was not sufficiently respectful. Shrines are usually very accepting spaces, so her reaction had disturbed me.[15] I could share the anger I felt toward that woman precisely because Rubab's notions of what it means to be a Pakistani woman come through so clearly in her writing. I knew she would sympathise, and, as a reader, I also knew of writers with whom I would not have comfortably raised this. This is because a certain form of conservative womanly comportment and individual views about it are so clear in their writings.

Rubab's work allows a glimpse into the political turmoil of the late 1970s through the vantage point of a young woman. However, because this is a fictional story rather than an autobiographical account, it allows her to reshape the moments she experienced. Moreover, this reworking is not just at the public level of events which were taking place around her but also at the private level of imagined possibilities of a woman's role in that scenario. Therefore, as she writes about Abeer, imagination, memory, ethics, and desires weave together. The novel is about a particular moment in Pakistan, and it is through her vantage point on what it was like to live as a young woman in those times. However, it also includes her desires (to see her daughter as a young woman) and ethics (ideas of how a woman should be). There is a certain reworking of both the inner (emotional landscapes or personal lives) and the outer (events taking place in the nation). Given the nature of this genre, there is also a very strong element of how a woman should act or behave. In other words, it is not just lived experiences but also how a woman should live those experiences.

In the previous paragraphs, I have shown how personal desires, lived moments in Pakistan's history, and notions of how a woman should behave texture these narratives. I will now share a 2003 digest story which depicts themes such as women's work empowerment and the dynamics of family and state. I will contextualise the story by connecting it to specific realities of women's paid employment in Pakistan and then share my own engagement with the same story as a digest reader.

'Shelter on Nameless Paths': A Digest Story

This particular digest story allows us a glimpse into women's lived experiences of institutions such as the state and family. Although the state provides certain basic rights, familial dynamics often determine the implementation of these legal rights. To give a simple example, legally, women are entitled to inheritance through the West Pakistan Muslim Personal Law (Shariat Act, 1962) and Muslim Family Law Ordinance (1961). However, many forgo this because of familial pressure. Therefore, although family is often a source of belonging and comfort, in certain instances it also becomes a site of deprivation. The story we will now explore allows us a glimpse into the daily lived reality of these dynamics through the contrast between the inner (family) and the outer (represented by work, guest, and readers). The plot is relatively simple: revolving around a woman named Saima who is under psychological pressure because of her husband.

'Have you even seen Sunny? The child is absolutely filthy.' Wasiq picked up his wallet from the TV trolley and glared at Saima.

'Oh no, I'd just changed his clothes—he's spilled all the yogurt on himself. I'll just change him in a moment after changing Honey's diaper.' She quickly picked up the two-month-old baby girl and took her to the bathroom.

'What do you have on the stove?' Wasiq yelled again. Milk had boiled over. Saima quickly cleaned up Honey, ran to the kitchen, and grew even more nervous. 'What kind of a woman are you? You put the milk to boil and left the kitchen.' Wasiq frowned at her.

'I was nearby, Wasiq, but then I heard Honey crying, and when I went to the bedroom, I realised her diaper was soiled. I became busy with that,' she nervously began explaining.

'And this—Sunny?' Wasiq sarcastically raised his finger toward the child. 'What matter of huge importance were you taking care of while he was dripping with yogurt? God knows when you'll learn some household skills; you're nothing but a lazy and incompetent woman. Managing this small house is an impossible task for you.' He kept grumbling as he ate his food.

'I try my best, Wasiq, but I don't know why mistakes still happen. Slowly, it will get better.'

'The hell it will get better! The ability that a person does not have, one should not even expect that it would develop. It's been two years since we've been married, but you haven't acquired a single quality, and it's my misfortune that I got married to you.' Wasiq sighed.

Saima felt ashamed. 'In these two years, we've also had one baby after another. First Sunny, and then, eleven months later, Honey. After the second birth, I lost my stamina; it's not easy taking care of two little children.'

'People have twin babies, and they manage them well. Yours aren't even twins, and you have all these excuses—as for the household tasks, you have a woman who cleans and washes clothes; all you need to do is cook.'

'Please try to understand, Wasiq.' She was ready to cry. 'It's not about the amount of work; it's about having time. Cooking hardly takes an hour, but with the children, I don't even get that. I start to peel onions, and Honey wakes up. I make the bottle for her, and during that time, Sunny becomes hungry. Making something for him, Cerelac, soup, or some other light food; making it, then feeding him, then bathing him—all this takes hours. Honey keeps waking up, and she keeps crying in between. She gets scared if I leave her alone, and if I leave Sunny with her, he tries to pick her up or play with her and in the process pulls her hands or feet, so she cries even more. He's a child—he doesn't know. I've asked you so many times to hire someone to help me with this.'

'Never—you just want to increase expenses for no reason; an extra mouth to feed, clothe, and give a monthly salary to.'

'Okay, let it be. You're getting late; change your clothes.' She changed the subject as she took off Sunny's clothes and began filling the tub with warm water for his bath.

'Haven't you ironed my white shirt?' Wasiq called from the bedroom.

'Oh no, I completely forgot! Sunny was running a fever yesterday, so I got busy with that, I'll just iron it now.'

Wasiq came out of the bedroom. She postponed Sunny's bath and rushed to iron the shirt.

'Now you'll spend an hour doing this.' He glanced at Sunny, who was on the floor without his clothes and had wet himself. Wasiq began shouting again. 'Are you trying to give him pneumonia? Early in the morning, you've left him naked on the cold floor. What kind of a woman are you?' He grew angrier.

'Let me just iron this shirt. I'll get to him in a minute.'

'You don't have the ability to even complete a little task properly.'

Saima tried her best to hold back her tears. She thought to herself, Ability? What ability don't I have? I learned so much, and yet this is how my life ended up. Am I the same person I was years ago? Life was carefree before marriage ... What had she achieved after marriage? Sarcasm, daily criticism, and an endless treadmill of running after children and the house. She always felt rushed, her infant daughter kept her awake at night, sleep deprivation had led to constant swelling of and redness in her eyes. Her face was withered and yellowed with fatigue. Tangled hair and unironed, soiled clothes [*mulgajay kapray*]. Could anyone say this was the same Saima who was known for how well she dressed? ...

Husbands in their husbandness constantly belittle women, and by rejecting them, degrading them, pacify their own insecurities. They tell their wives about their previous relationships, brag about their 'colourful' past, and savour revealing those details to their wives, belittling them, and if they hear even a little thing about their wife's past, they become suspicious and keep pinching them with the arrows of suspicion and sarcasm. They hurt their wife's self-respect to their heart's content, burn it, and see it withered [*jalaatay hain sulghaatay hain*]. And they themselves share their own stories of conquest as a matter of pride and masculinity.

Although there are financial constraints, she lacks access even to the resources they have. For instance, as readers, we learn that they have a small car, gifted by Saima's family, but Saima herself never gets to use it because Wasiq does not let her. She herself

uses public transportation and suggests selling the car to meet
household expenses, but Wasiq is not willing to put himself in any
discomfort. Things begin to change when Saima interacts with
her house-guest.

Najma bhabhi was a strong woman with strong nerves. She had
begun noticing Saima's routine. 'Our age difference is so much
that I would prefer to call you my daughter.' Saima was done with
household tasks and was putting Honey to bed when Najma bhabhi
walked in. Wasiq and Akmal sahib (her husband) were in the
drawing room, drinking tea.

'You can call me whatever you prefer,' Saima said pleasantly.
Honey was asleep now, so she began making milk for Sunny.

'Daughter, you're educated, and from your behaviour, I know
you have a very calm [*suljhee hui*], wise nature. I don't expect a girl
like you to be so unwise. The first child—it's okay. God blessed
you quickly, but after that it was the responsibility of both of you
to be careful. Let alone two years—you didn't even leave a gap of
two months. I don't need to tell you that such a little gap between
births affects both the mother and the baby. And why should the
first child's attention, milk, and tending he requires be shared with
another?

'I understand this, bhabhi.' She lowered her head. 'But Wasiq
didn't agree, and I couldn't go against his will.'

'This is your lack of understanding. Why can't you change his
will?'

'He does whatever he thinks best.'

'Why are you treating yourself this way? You're educated!
What do you lack? You can also think well and decide well for
your family. When you have these abilities, why not express them
openly?'

'And if one is not even given a chance to express them?' She
sighed and looked into Najma bhabhi's eyes. There was a look of
despondency on her face.

'Then one should find that chance. Why are you putting yourself
through this kind of self-pity and self-abuse? You've only been
married for two years, and looking at you, it seems as if it's been

decades. Don't make yourself so worthless, daughter. Times have changed; women who lose themselves in their households are not praised but made fun of. What do you think, by constantly pandering to every need of your husband and children, one day you'll get some big reward? That's not the way it works.

'The husband thinks this kind of care is his right and receives it without any acknowledgement or appreciation. The woman hears sarcastic remarks about her foolishness till her old age, and when she grows old and looks toward her grown-up children, they too don't respect her. From their childhood they've seen their father degrading their mother, so unconsciously they too begin to see her as worthless and don't share their joys or sorrows with her.

'You should live in a way that both your husband and your children realise your importance in their lives, and for this, it is necessary that you stand on your own feet. Make use of your education and find work. This way, your own personality will shine, and the family members too will see your time and routine as important. Obviously, when the financial responsibility lessens on the man, he too will have a kinder attitude—it will be to his own benefit. Third, in a time of need, you won't be dependent on your husband or your children. Instead, you'll be able to support them ....'

Najma bhabhi left on the third day, but it was as if she had left a guiding light for her. Secretly, Saima began to explore jobs advertised in the newspaper. By now, Honey was six months old and Sunny a year and a half. Her in-laws lived fifteen minutes away. She realised that she could leave the children there and go to a job. In any case, Honey had to be fed from a bottle because her own health didn't provide enough milk for breastfeeding.

'What is this? Am I going to have to eat rice and lentils for dinner?' Wasiq shouted.

'I went for a haircut,' she answered, as if Wasiq's anger was of no consequence.

'Why isn't my tea here yet?'

'I was using a facial mask. I'll make tea for you now if you'll take care of the baby,' she replied.

Wasiq lost his temper and launched into his usual lecture about Saima's laziness and inefficiency. Saima remained silent and then nodded her head in agreement.

'You're right; I'm not only lazy but also ill-mannered.' What could Wasiq say? Everything he wanted to say had already been said.

Gradually, he began to see that his criticism no longer had any effect on Saima. She was not afraid of his outbursts anymore.

A few weeks later, she informs him that she has found employment.

'How will you work? Who will run the house?'

'But you say yourself it's the cleaning lady who runs the house. I don't do anything, so she will continue to run the house,' said Saima.

When a woman is dependent on her husband for money, she can't rebel [*sarkashi nahi aati*], but once she becomes financially independent, she changes ….

After many arguments and threats, Saima still stuck to her decision, and Wasiq had to bend to her will. Deep down, he wasn't as strong or solid as Saima's appeasement [*jee huzoori*] had led him to believe. It was just flaky intimidation, and it didn't withstand her determination. Moreover, seven thousand rupees (her salary) was a substantial amount, and deep down, he realised that many household expenses could easily be met through it.

Saima began working. They would both leave together; she would drop off her children at her in-laws', and Wasiq would drop her at her workplace. In the afternoon he would pick her up; they would have food at the in-laws' and return home. The minute she reached home, she would busy herself with household tasks and taking care of the children.

When Saima received her first salary, she bought clothes for the children, and for the first time after her marriage, she bought something for herself: two pairs of shoes, an imported shampoo, and some items of makeup.

Wasiq lost his temper when he saw this. 'In her greed, this woman has wasted away all her income in one day. If you've started earning, put it into the bank so it will be useful for the future.'

'Wasiq, it's good to plan for the future, but it doesn't mean that one should ignore one's necessities and makes one's present a time of frustration and continual deprivation.'

When Saima receives her first salary, she also hires a young girl to help with the children. When Wasiq asks her about it, she tells him that because the maid's salary will come out of her pay, she didn't feel the need to ask him. Eventually, Wasiq realises that he can no longer intimidate her, and Saima leads a happy and busy life.

DIGEST FICTION AS A SITE OF FLUID LIVED REALITIES

What are the key themes in this story, and how do they depict lived realities? Within the circle of Saima's family, we see one-sided relationships. There are only three primary figures: her two children and her husband, and in these relationships, constant demands are placed on her. Saima loves her children, but tending to them is often overwhelming. Their presence is demanding but silent, whereas her husband's presence is both critical and demanding. Thus, neither her children nor her husband are sources of emotional nurturing. In contrast to these insiders (family figures), as outsiders (readers and/or audience), we are privy to her physical exhaustion as well as her emotional turmoil. The readers become a silent listening ear or an invisible gazing eye as she shares her problems of sleep deprivation, feelings of inadequacy, and being devalued. The other sympathetic figure is again an outsider, the house-guest. Our gaze as readers is magnified when we see the house-guest validating what we have been invited to observe. The house-guest (and the readers) recognise Saima's intrinsic talent, and it is through the validation of this outsider, the house-guest, that she feels strong enough to take a stand for herself at home.

In other words, rather than the inner circle of her family, it's the outside that restores Saima's sense of intrinsic worth and validation. This pattern continues as she rapidly finds acceptance in the workplace (when she obtains paid work), again a validation of her worth, whereas her husband continues to reject her through his criticism. Toward the end, as we hear her schedule; it is noticeable that her husband, who did not allow her to use the car (hence her reliance on public transport), now picks her up and drops her at her workplace—a subtle change in the power dynamic between the two—a consequence of the income she now earns. Thus, the outside (workplace validation, financial remuneration) helps establish her worth within her home.

The reality of paid employment is, of course, fraught with far more pressures and problems than that which this story depicts. Rather than a depiction of reality, the way employment changes Saima's life is reflective of a kind of hope or promise of public-sphere participation reflective of the early 2000s. This story was written and published in 2003, during the initial period of a military government headed by Musharraf (1999–2008). To set himself apart from the retrogressive regime represented by the previous military dictator (Zia), Musharraf announced several steps to increase women's participation in the public sphere. These included reserving 33 per cent of the seats in parliament for women and making policy changes that led to over 400 women counsellors entering the public sphere. As policy changes created opportunity, the effects of economic liberalisation, such as inflation, forced many middle-class families to avail themselves of these opportunities and allow their women to join the workforce. In a sense, the acceptability and usefulness of working women began to increase in the middle class. To give a concrete example of these changed perceptions, in her 2002 interview with me, *Pakeeza*'s editor, Ansar, highlighted that one of the significant changes she had observed was in terms of readers' and writers' perceptions of working women—not just in fictional representations, but also in real life. Whereas previously women who were looking for daughters-in-law would ask Ansar for a homely girl, now they increasingly asked for a working woman who could share financial responsibility with their sons (Ahmed, 2004).

For women themselves, this possibility of ease in economic pressures also held the promise of validation and a more assertive role at home. Saima's story depicts this particular promise of being viewed as worthy by her family because of her empowerment through paid work. Thus, the story presents a localised, specific form of the popular notion of women's unpaid work as traditional and patriarchal and paid work as modern and emancipated. As a 2001 study on Pakistani women's workplace empowerment points out, the fulfilment of this promise depends upon several other factors, such as marital position and class.[16] Thus, while paid employment holds a promise, its fulfilment is not guaranteed. Some respondents did speak about increasing inclusiveness in decision-making and an increasing significance in the home; for others, this was not the case. In other words, paid employment did not automatically lead to empowerment; factors such as marital position, class, and family dynamics determined that. Yet, for many working middle-class women whose mothers had not worked, paid employment held the promise of an independent identity, validation at home, and greater respect. Indeed, this hope is reflected in the story, as we see in Saima's life as her circumstances begin changing.

Let me now turn to the role of body in this story. The sense of control over Saima's life begins and ends with the body in a very interesting way. We are introduced to Saima's life through a kind of embodied daily domesticity (rushing over to the kitchen, tending to her children's bodily needs of being cleaned and fed). A key conversation with the house-guest is also about bodily control as Saima confides to her that having children in quick succession was not her decision. In this sense, even though she has the responsibility of caring for the children, the authority of how many children to have and when is not hers. Therefore, at the beginning of the story, her body is not really her own.

As things begin to change, the initial expressions of defiance are again around the body: for instance, putting a beauty mask on her face instead of cooking dinner. Similarly, the objects she buys on her first shopping trip include shoes, clothes, imported shampoo, and some items of makeup. This could, of course, also be read as consumerist longings, but I find it significant that none of the objects is related to the household. Moreover, although 'some clothes for the children' is casually related, the specificity of imported shampoo, clothes, and two new pairs of shoes conveys a sense of savoured pleasure. Thus, at the beginning of the story, it is an abject, disrespected body which is denied basic needs such as sleep and rest, both by Saima's husband and Saima herself. The recasting of notions of self is also through her changed attitude toward her own body as she begins to pamper it with consumer goods. The very last line of the story brings us full circle: 'What a contrast between that sluggish Saima and this well-dressed, active Saima [*Kahan voh jhalanga si* Saima *aur kahan ye* smart *bani phurtheeli si* Saima].'

It is also interesting that rather than convincing her husband to help with housework, Saima instead hires a maid to ease her domestic and childcare responsibilities, which points to a class dynamic. The feminist scholar Chandra Mohanty correctly highlights that ideologies of womanhood are not entirely based on gender, but also on class and race. Gender and class are both relational terms, and it is the intersection of various systemic networks of class and race, sexuality, and nation that position us as women (Mohanty, 1991: 51). Similarly, here too Saima's sense of housework being a never-ending treadmill does not result in any fundamental redistribution of these responsibilities within her family but instead leads to a power dynamic with another woman from an underprivileged class.

Near the beginning of the story, we learn of a maid who cleans and washes clothes for Saima's household. We neither hear nor see her; class solidarity trumps gender as Saima opens up to Najma bhabhi, but the maid's presence is felt only in terms of the tussle between Saima and her husband regarding the degree of housework pressure. In a sense, there are two women who witness Saima's life, Najma bhabhi and the maid, but only one is vocal and visible. In the same way, the new maid's presence is also silent and invisible. In one of the sections I had to cut, for the sake of brevity, readers are introduced to her as Ayesha, the twelve-year-old daughter of a maid who works nearby, but Ayesha herself remains silent and invisible. Hiring her is a symbolic gesture of independence, but one that is embroiled in various entanglements of class. In this sense, Saima is able to continue her paid employment because a twelve-year-old body is obliged by poverty and circumstances to work for her.

In the preceding few paragraphs, I have explored this story as a window into certain contemporary realities. Let me now share my engagement with this story as a digest reader.

SELF-REFLEXIVE ENGAGEMENT AS A READER

As the youngest of eight, I had access to (and read) varying reading material which my siblings had accumulated. The digest genre was not represented, as no one in my immediate family read them. I discovered them in my early teens when I spent summer vacations at an aunt's house. Noticing my interest, she gave me a bundle to take back home. I began to spend hours reading them in the face of family disapproval. A clear memory is of my mother flipping through a digest and exasperatedly asking, 'What's in it? Is it even appropriate for you?' and my defensive fifteen-year-old self, pointing out the words printed on the cover: 'For young women and girls.' I continued to read digests but rarely disclosed this interest. I often took part in discussions of European or Latin American literature or English fiction by South Asian novelists. An individual's choice of reading material defines his/her personality, so interest in certain genres was proudly disclosed and interest in others less openly. One of the reasons was the Urdu–English class divide.

In Pakistan, a person's command over English, the ability to read it (or speak it), is a class marker, as the elite and upper-middle-class mostly use English. Moreover, engagement with English fiction is also an indicator of being part of a wider international discourse.

There are voices which advocate a disavowal of English, arguing that it is a colonial language, and instead promote Urdu, the national language.[17] This standpoint too is not without problems as it often entails privileging Urdu over other regional languages. Moreover, Urdu's dominance of the cultural centre has led to a sense of marginalisation amongst other linguistic groups, in turn leading to a strengthening of ethnic nationalism, regional identities, and a national culture that does not allow any real space for diverse voices (Ali, 2003: 128).

Even within Urdu fiction, there is a dichotomy, as certain genres of Urdu literature are prized, while others, such as those published in digests, are seen as lowbrow and frivolous. In other words, although engagement with Urdu literature is seen as a marker of being cultured, digest reading is positioned as buying into retrogressive, socially constituted norms of being a 'good' Eastern/Pakistani woman. Therefore, like many other digest readers, I shared my interest with few people and positioned it as an activity that was pleasurable but contradictory to the values I held as a feminist.

After a few years, I faced an emotionally challenging time. There were few spare hours; I worked full-time at a non-profit organisation, and the evenings were spent taking care of my children. In this context, I had to be selective about reading material and found myself gravitating toward digests. This was partly because, given the short page length and the simplicity of expression of these stories, they were easy to fit into the little time I had for reading. Besides, it required little mental effort, and because all work-related reading and writing was in English, it was refreshing to switch to reading Urdu at the end of the day.

Gradually, it became a daily ritual. After putting the children to bed and organising things for the next day, I would settle in and read about other women and their lives. It became a space where I could be by myself and refuse the daily obligations which work and familial responsibilities entailed. This is similar to what the literary theorist Janice Radway calls a 'declaration of independence'. Romance reading is not just about textual narratives but is often positioned by readers as an event that allows them to temporarily refuse the demands of their familial responsibilities while at the same time providing fictional companionship and conversation (1984: 11).[18] Moreover, through reading, women are able to vicariously attend to and take responsibility for their own requirements as independent individuals who require emotional sustenance and solicitude (1984: 93) without posing a 'fundamental challenge' to the balance of power (1984: 103).

As a reader, my engagement with digest fiction was deeply conflicted in several ways. It was a site that centred desire around marriage, familial bliss, and heterosexual romance. Yet there were also counter-narratives within this form. In other words, rather than a monolithic reiteration of heterosexual notions of romance, there were also stories that wove in the same domestic details and familial everydayness but pointed to a certain disillusionment. For instance, although most stories ended with a woman achieving male validation through patience, appeasement, or her genuine love for her partner, there were also stories (such as the one shared earlier) that challenged the socially constituted norms of marital or familial bliss and adopted the framework of achieving validation through assertion or financial empowerment. In these stories, there really were no heroes but simply ordinary, irritable men who were critical and often grew insecure. Rather than nurturing heroes, in these stories, the sense of companionship was provided by the fictional women being subjected to these circumstances. In each scenario, rather than explaining her inner feelings to the man with whom she was in conflict, she shared it with the readers.[19] Thus, the same genre that centred fulfilment on romance or male companionship was also a site for a counter-narrative of disillusionment with the very same notions.

As a reader, I found myself gravitating toward stories which were about married life and its conflicts. These stories were largely about everyday domesticity and the ordinary. There were no grand ideas behind them, and I often did not agree with the ending. Yet, notwithstanding this, there was a sense of belonging through a shared experiential knowledge of the everyday, inner dialogues, and familiar geography (such as specific markets around the city) depicted in these stories. Moreover, as a reader, rather than engaging with fiction as such, my engagement was primarily with particular writers whose personal lives were familiar to me. In other words, the stories were perceived as self-expression penned by a familiar woman whose rhythms of daily life and circumstances resonated with mine. In this sense, fiction was not in a vacuum, in and of itself. Given readers' familiarity with writers' personal lives, there was a sense of shared experiential knowledge and sentiments conveyed through these stories.

In this context, the previous story, by the author Shazia Chaudhary, was especially evocative. As a reader, I knew the broad contours of her life through her published letters in the readers' section as well as interviews. This included details such as the particulars of playful banter with her siblings, her parent's worries about her academics because of her writing in digests, and anecdotes about college life. Pictures of her wedding and children were also public, along with personal details such as her daily routine, her children's habits, and the rhythm of her day. As a reader, I did not like her earlier work which was mostly about heterosexual romance, but after her marriage her stories about romance underwent a change, and increasingly her writing became about being in an unsatisfactory relationship. These were desires that remained unfulfilled in her actual life, as the middle-class norms of respectability prescribe arranged marriages. In this context, fiction perhaps became a way of vicariously living these experiences without posing a fundamental challenge to predominant familial norms. Subsequently, fiction also became a gateway where she could openly voice her disillusionment about certain experiential realties and make her private sentiments public, without getting into any open conflicts or confrontations.

The changed demeanour in her photographs and the themes in her stories reflected the self-doubt I was experiencing at the time. The story was not necessarily a self-disclosure but a shared private feeling I could relate to. Thus, feelings such as anxiety, hopelessness, or emotional frustration were shared as I felt them by reading about the fictional Saima.

Given the context in which I worked (the gender unit of a non-profit organisation) during the day, I dealt with facts about violence against women, power dynamics, and lack of access to resources, and in the evening I found a degree of closure by accompanying a fictional character on her journey to a destination that provided validation in one way or another. I particularly enjoyed reading Saima's story. Perhaps more than anything else, there was the fluid domesticity, a kind of embodied existence, which was enjoyable. The daily details of milk that had to be boiled, babies that had to be bathed, and bottles that had to be heated were comfortingly familiar. In some sense, the specific telling of each embodied action privileged these daily maintenance tasks of motherhood and housework that often remain unseen.

The values of fulfilment through work, gestures of assertion as a woman (beyond the roles of wife and mother), resonated with my own views. There was also a vicarious pleasure in reading about Saima's gestures of defiance and the sense of frustration that shifts from her to her husband. Given editorial concerns about not being seen as a challenge to the fundamental balance of power within the familial setting, published digest stories often carry the message of appeasement rather than assertion. A typical theme is that of an indifferent or outright abusive man who gradually changes and begins to love a woman because of her patience and forbearance. Thus, 'to win a heart through acts of service' (*khidmat se dil jeet laina*) is a common term within this genre. In this context, seeing Saima assert herself and her individuality provided a certain reshaping. The long paragraphs about Saima's resentment and bitterness are not just about Wasiq but also about socially constituted norms. Saima's behaviour in the first half of the story reflects dominant norms of being a 'good' (digest) wife, such as not responding and not being confrontational. In the beginning she is the kind of woman who hopes to win her husband's love through service. However, the promise held by digest norms about winning his validation never materialises, and therefore the despondency in response to Najma bhabhi's question, 'So you think one day you'll find some reward for this service?' To a reader who is familiar with this genre, Najma bhabhi's visit marked a sort of rupture, a retelling through assertion and confidence rather than appeasement and sacrifice. In that sense, the story questioned these notions (through the very genre that played a key role in articulating these norms in the first place). For me, as a reader, there was a sense of shared response, a mutual disillusionment that the promise of conciliation and sacrifice was just that—a promise—and another way had to be found to navigate these roles. The story provided a navigational map through a fictional witnessing of how Saima begins asserting herself.

Turning again to the writer, although Shazia Chaudhary's fictional characters lived the lives they sought, her own came to an abrupt and tragic end at the age of twenty-eight. She had begun tutoring children to supplement her husband's income. One afternoon, she asked her husband to drop her off. On the way, he lost control of the motorcycle, and they had an accident. He himself escaped unhurt, but Shazia Chaudhary went into a coma and died three days later, leaving behind a one-year-old daughter and a two-year-old son. When they brought back her bag from the accident site, they also found a note in her handwriting addressed to the stranger who might find it, giving her name and her parents' contact number, which indicates that she had somehow sensed an accident might occur.[20]

Her death was announced on the digest cover through a close-up of her as a bride and bold letters that exclaimed 'Shazia Chaudhary, *Aah*'.[21] Letters printed inside provided details of how various readers found out about her accident, the kinds of prayers they arranged, and then the grief and shock at losing her. Like myself, very few of the readers had ever met her. A simplistic reading could be in terms of the grief we feel when we hear of someone's passing away whose work we admire. However, in this context, it seemed to go beyond that. As a reader, I felt the loss much more deeply. Partly, there was the sense of loss of a voice which had provided fictional companionship during quiet evenings as well as a sense of validity regarding what I felt.

The outpouring of grief in readers' letters that continued to follow the news of her death also brought home the fact that many other readers had connected with her stories as I had. Shazia Chaudhary herself was not able to change her circumstances but her stories were a bridge that temporarily connected certain readers to a shared sense of disillusionment. Readers' engagements with the digest genre or fiction itself vary, and my experience cannot be generalised. I have shared it to highlight how engagement as a reader can bestow a sense of connection and belonging during periods of alienation. Experiencing a divorce was an alienating experience for me, accompanied by legal problems, social disapproval, and familial conflict. In this context, certain stories in this genre became a source of validating feelings I was ambivalent about. There were, of course, other factors; digest fiction was not the only source of relationality or support but it was one of them.

TESTING BOUNDARIES OF KNOWN WORLDS

My engagement as a reader can partly be contextualised by briefly turning to the literary theorist Lynn Hapgood (2005). She positions garden romance novels (novels with a garden setting) which women wrote and read for themselves as a late Victorian and early twentieth century response to the modern. In this context, she points to the 'spills' that such genres can take in individual lives as she states:

> At any point of personal need, hope, or fear, women could try out possible alternative reactions through the medium of romance novels, in which they knew that their concerns would always be firmly located at the centre of the stage (Hapgood, 2005: 121).[22]

Shazia Chaudhary's earlier characters that embodied notions of romance and desire did not resonate with me as a reader. However, Saima's life echoed certain experiences. I suggest that, given the affective nature of bonds in this community (which I discussed in the previous chapter), some of these texts become metaphorical dwelling places, resting areas of comfort and solace. Just as a house is not its windows, doors, or roof but rather a combination of all these parts, similarly, here, too, a particular combination of various factors, such as familiarity with the writer, shared emotional knowledge, and particular circumstances of a reader's life, can and do lead to the appropriation of specific stories as metaphorical dwelling places.

The story by Shazia Chaudhary which I first read in 2003 was one that spoke about assertion rather than appeasement. Twelve years later as I read it again, it becomes one of embodiment and the dichotomy of public and private. In both cases, the spectre of Shazia Chaudhary writing this story and creating imagined possibilities for herself continues to loom large in the background. The affective texture of this community and the personal details that readers know about the writers' lives make this engagement a form of interweaving that goes beyond text and reader. Derrida's analogy of text as a blank cheque left on the sidewalk is apt in this context. These stories too are blank cheques left by writers which individual readers pick up and to which they ascribe different values. As a digest reader, my engagement with this specific story led to an intellectual exploration of this genre, and thirteen years later, as I write these lines, the story still forms a part of this journey.

To reiterate, this chapter demonstrates how digest fiction reflects lived realities and imagined possibilities—both of attachments in the digest community as well as the larger dynamics of living as a woman in contemporary Pakistan—and how individual readers appropriate certain stories within the specificity of their personal circumstances. As anthropologists we are required to live in the spaces in which our respondents live. Our ethnographies describe the sights, smells, and sounds of those places to evoke a sense of what it is like to be there. The community of digest readers and writers does not have a shared spatiality. I could write about the digest office, libraries, or even the homes visited or lived in during fieldwork, but that is not really where they dwell. Their dwellings are these stories: metaphorical worlds which are created and inhabited in a variety of ways. These arise from emotions, desires, and experiences and carry an entanglement of presence and absence. In the first short story, Seema's absence allows Uneeza to create (bring to presence) her fictional husband and child. Their shared emotional world and friendship are strengthened through distance. Presence (physical proximity) causes it to disappear. In the context of writers, Rubab's' daughter is absent, but she brings her to presence by creating the characters of Abeer and her mother. Similarly, Shazia Chaudhary brings to presence the imagined possibility of empowerment through paid employment. In this sense, they have both reworked their given lives and brought to presence another world based on imagined possibilities. Readers, in turn, inhabit these fictional worlds and sometimes appropriate them as metaphorical dwelling places.

The German philosopher Martin Heidegger suggests that Plato and the birth of metaphysics led to the notion of knowledge as clarity. The object of studying something became to make it clear and distinct. However, in pursuing clarity, we often lose sight of the mystery and weight that any phenomenon carries. In that context, this chapter has been about exploring the mystery of these little worlds that form and surround simple stories of domesticity.

NOTES

1. Amna Mohani, 'Tasavvur ki Parchhaiyan (Shadows of Imagination)', *Pakeeza*, 1974.
2. For details, *see* Sacks, Oliver (2010), *The Mind's Eye*.
3. As I became close to certain writers, flattering text messages addressing me as 'the one who lives in my heart (*janam*)' became a usual part of the interaction.
4. *Khawateen Digest* (1979), Letters section.
5. '*Humain bhi Jeenay Do* (Let Us Live)', *Pakeeza*, October 1973.
6. Feroza Begum, 'The Other Side of the Picture (*Tasveer ka rukh*)', *Pakeeza*, October 1973.
7. The movie centres around two women (Jamila and Razia) who are close friends. When one of them moves to a different city, they continue their friendship through letters. The way they address each other in these letters is similar to the endearments described in the digest story. However, their letters never reach each other because of Jamila's brother. He neither posts his sister's letters nor gives her those written by Razia. Jamila ends up faking an illness so her parents will send her to live with Razia. However, the doctor who comes in to treat her falls in love with her, and she gets engaged to him. On the day of the wedding, he has an accident and dies, which causes Jamila to lose her mental balance. Her parents send her to a different city for treatment, where she meets the doctor's older brother. Because they look very similar, she assumes this is her fiancé and wants him to marry her. Razia comes back into the picture when we discover that the wife to whom he wants to remain loyal is Razia. Once Razia finds out about Jamila, she convinces the doctor to marry her, and they all live together (Ali, 2014).
   The movie won five President's Medals for various categories, as well as Nigar Awards, one of the highest film awards in Pakistan. Its popularity and success at the box office indicate its resonance with the public. Nonetheless, it was also critiqued in liberal circles as encouraging polygamy.

8. Kamran Asdar Ali, 'On Female Friendships', *Dawn*, 3 August 2014 <http://www.dawn.com/news/1122839>.

9. Social constructionists, represented by Butler (but also including other feminists such as Spivak), do not position the body as biologically given. They are concerned with the 'lived body' as it is represented and used in different cultures. They problematise mind–body dualism and argue that there is no 'pure body' as such. Bodies are always caught up in social structures (Grosz, 1994: 10–21). In this context, Butler's primary concern is the underlying grid of gendered normativity. As she writes:

   > What continues to concern me most is the following kinds of questions: what will and what will not constitute an intelligible life, and how the presumptions about normative gender and sexuality determine in advance what will qualify as the 'human' and the 'livable'? In other words, how do normative gender presumptions work to delimit the very field of description that we have for the human? (Butler, 1999: xxii)

10. Although performance implies playing the part of a character, performativity for Butler derives from linguistics and refers to utterances, acts, or sets of acts that produce the effect they name. In framing gender as performative, Butler argues that gender formation is a continuing and ongoing performance through which our maleness or femaleness becomes intelligible. There is no essence that is being expressed; rather, gender is performative because it brings into existence what it names or enacts. Thus, it requires repeated performance that is generated through bodily gestures, movements, and styles.

11. She develops this notion in the context of her ethnographic work on biological females in West Sumatra, commonly known as tombois, who adopt masculinity.

12. There have been few studies on this genre within Pakistan, and those which have been conducted reinforce the social perception of these digests as frivolous. See Pervez (1984) and Ahmar (1997).

13. Publicly, they acted indifferent, while privately, they supplied their teachers with daily necessities and acted as a channel between them and their families.

14. Interview with writer, Islamabad, June 2012.

15. In Pakistan, women's attire varies greatly, from abayas that cover the bodily contours completely and are accompanied by a tight scarf to jeans or shalwar kameez with the head uncovered. It is common to see these in public spaces and shrines, so her reaction to some of my hair showing stood out as a disturbing recent development.

16. Saba Gul Khattak, 'Women Work and Empowerment', In *Women's Work and Empowerment Issues in an Era of Economic Liberalisation: A Case study of*

Pakistan's Urban Manufacturing Sector. (ed.) Khattak, Saba Gul, and Asad Sayeed, 2001.

17. Pakistan's national language is Urdu. However, there are also several regional languages. Twelve per cent of the population speak Sindhi (mainly in south-eastern Sindh province); 48 per cent speak Punjabi, mainly in eastern Punjab province; 10 per cent speak Saraiki, a variant of Punjabi; 8 per cent speak Pashto, in west and north-western Pakistan; 8 per cent speak Urdu; 3 per cent speak Balochi, mainly in Balochistan <http://www.bbc.com/news/world-asia-34215293>, accessed on 15 September 2015.

18. Radway highlights this in the context of her ethnographic study of Western readers of romance and shares that during the initial phase, her guiding question was how readers interpret texts. She, however, began realising that respondents positioned her question of what romance novels meant for them by talking about romance reading as an activity in their everyday lives (1984: 7).

19. Radway suggests that despite being happily married, the readers' need for nurturing was not met adequately within their day-to-day existence. For instance, the novels liked most by the readers were those where the hero was more or less androgynous in his style of caring in terms of maternal concern, and nurturing. In this sense, romance reading permitted the ritual retelling of the psychic process through which traditional heterosexuality was constructed for women, but it also appeared to exist as a protest against the fundamental inability of heterosexuality to satisfy the very desires with which it engendered women. Thus, one of her key arguments is that for women, romance reading is a 'profoundly conflicted activity centered upon a profoundly conflicted form' (1984: 14).

20. Telephonic interview with Shazia's friend, July 2012.

21. *Aah* and *haai* are both expressions of dismay and sadness.

22. Hapgood argues that such genres have a contractual nature in which the reader becomes an affective participant in an open-ended fictional discourse, and meanings are negotiated between the writer and reader. Thus, the writer forsakes the self-affirmation of the detachment to explore, mediate, or create 'imaginative proving grounds' for their readers' experience. In this sense, 'Fiction empowers women to be heroines in their own scripts and to test the boundaries of their known world.' (Hapgood, 2005: 123).

3

In Quest of Meaning: Four Women
and their Stories

This chapter continues the trajectory of the earlier ones by examining how different writers depict and engage with the same lived realities. It does so by focusing on four digest writers who come from the same family and live in a shared household. I draw on Edward Said (1983), who aptly asserts the importance of contextualising texts in the worlds through which they emerge. He highlights that texts are not written in a vacuum and argues that although textual analysis through psychoanalytic or Marxist theory yields valuable insights, it also leads to a certain form of rootlessness. This is because texts are analysed in and of themselves, rather than in tandem with the larger realities of power and discourse that permeate the world to which the authors belong. In this context, I highlight the world of these writers and trace how each of them engages with the given world through her own lens. Specifically, I explore two concepts: agency and engagement.

All four writers are remarkable; although familial norms have not allowed them mobility and education, as digest writers they have succeeded both in achieving literacy and a kind of mobility by making their private voices public. As one of them shared, 'I could not become a lawyer or a social worker but sitting at home I could write stories and become a digest writer.' Thus, writing fiction for digests has become an avenue for agency in the absence of spatial mobility and formal education. This chapter explores the notion of agency by demonstrating the variety of forms it has taken in each writer's life. I draw on the anthropologist Saba Mahmood (2001), who asserts that agency understood as the capacity to realise one's own interests against the weight of obstacles is only one standpoint; there can be other culturally specific forms of it. I demonstrate that even within the same context of prescribed norms and daily lives, agency can assume different meanings. Although all four digest writers live within the same prescribed framework of familial norms, and each has engaged with fiction writing as an avenue for self-expression, the connotations of this voice and the agency it provides are very different for each. Furthermore, I draw on the anthropologist Lila Abu Lughod (2000), as her reflections on resistance allow us to go beyond the framework of 'resistance' as valid only if it overturns power structures.

Besides, in the context of engagements with the world, I discuss that although their bodies have restricted mobility, given their position as faith healers and spiritual leaders, these women often witness or undergo experiences that defy mainstream bounds of reality. Through an ethnographic account of my stay with them, I explore how my own assumptions about reality and belief were occasionally overturned as I witnessed their experiences. The larger point I want to make here is that notwithstanding restricted mobility, they have unfettered time and often engage with the world through particular vantage points that are inaccessible to some of us.

This chapter has three strands. One is the story of these four women's lives as they narrated it; the second is their fiction, and the third is my own understanding of their lives and stories. The chapter begins with my initial perception of them as women in a remote Sindhi village who were 'oppressed' by their restricted mobility. I expand on how my perceptions (both about Sindh and their lives as Sindhi women) began to change through continuing contact and familiarity with their domesticity and everyday existence. The larger point I want to make here is how connections between women's private lives allow a kind of bridge that crosses over the otherness of class and ethnic differences. In other words, the two years of continuing contact with them over the phone allowed me a window into their everyday lives, and this everydayness changed rural Sindh from an unknown and unsafe place to my friends' home even before I visited it.

The second section begins by contextualising the family and the role digests play in their everyday lives and proceeds to these writers' narratives. Their writing and narration of their lives is not just raw material here but, as the literary theorist Barbara Harlow points out in the context of prison writings, 'It is in itself an articulation of a critical perspective' (1992: xi). This articulation is critical because frequently the stories we tell ourselves (or others) about our lives shape us in substantial ways. They of course correspond with actual facts or events, but how we choose to frame them into a narrative creates certain themes that shape the world (and our lives) for us. Thus, rather than filtering their narratives, I have presented them within the themes that they offered themselves. Expressed more simply, I have shared narratives as they were narrated. Key questions in this section include: How does each writer see her engagement with fiction? What are the stories that are important for each writer, and how does each see her stories as linking her everyday life, conflicting desires, and motivations?

The third section presents my understanding of their trajectories and explores the theme of agency within the context of mobility, authenticity, and the dynamics of power and resistance. It explores questions such as: how can social challenges carry a productive force? What are the effects of restricted mobility on creative writing in this specific context? How can disengagement be a form of agency?

'INTERIOR' SINDH

Let us begin with my initial perception. My first introduction to these writers was through an editor. 'You should interview these women; they are from a respected religious family in Sindh and learned to write and read despite restricted mobility.' The words 'remote village in Sindh' conjured up a mental image of dark rooms with ornate furniture and gold-laden women resisting institutional structures of patriarchy by writing about their lives of restricted mobility. Over the next two years, as we got to know each other through long phone conversations, I became familiar with the sounds of their household: laughing children, rapid conversations in Sindhi, and some sense of the liveliness that surrounded them began to permeate my perception of their lives.

By the time I began to plan my trip to their village, it had become a visit to my friends Simran and Kulsoom's home (fictitious names). However, for my mother, it continued to be unknown and led to several concerns. 'You've never met them—how can you stay alone in their house? Take your sister with you.'

'That's not permitted in the rules for fieldwork.' I deployed the usual excuse I had when all else appeared to fail.

'But it's in interior Sindh—how will you go there by yourself?'

Her concerns held several layers. Never having met this family was just one; the fact that they lived in an area commonly referred to as 'interior Sindh' was another. One of the five provinces of Pakistan, in population, Sindh is the second largest and in area, the third largest. Its urban capital, Karachi (largely populated by Urdu-speaking Mohajirs), is socially perceived to be cosmopolitan. However, given the dynamics of ethnicity and language politics, rural Sindh is often referred to as 'interior Sindh'. In popular perception, in particular where I lived in Islamabad—the federal capital—rural Sindh was seen as unsafe, a place of armed robberies, kidnappings, and bandits. Thus, although she was comfortable with my trips to another continent (the US), this trip to another Pakistani province had her deeply worried.

We finally reached a compromise when a Sindhi friend, Abdul Haque, arranged for his family to pick me up from the bus stop and take me to the nearby city of Hyderabad where Simran's brother would pick me up. I was not looking forward to the twenty-three-hour bus journey from Islamabad. However, as is usually the case, the process itself held lessons for me which I expected only from the destination. The bus journey was a means to an end—a way of reaching the village—but the ride itself was as interesting (and insightful) as the destination. My mother's anxieties and my own lack of concern about going to Sindh had puzzled me. However, during the bus ride, I began realising that the conversations with the Sindhi writers had transformed it for me from an unknown place to my friends' home.

Let me share an ethnographic note from the bus ride to explain what I mean.

'*Aap idhar aa jaen inn khatoon ke saath, yahan* male assigned *hain*' (Please move next to the seat with that lady; a man has been mistakenly assigned the seat next to yours). Exasperated, I picked up my bags and switched seats for the third (or was it the fourth?) time. I moved next to a woman I came to know later as Yasmeen. Her face covered with a black veil, she moved her little daughter from the empty seat and welcomed me with a nod. She shared that the bus driver was her brother, and she was going to a city in southern Punjab called Rahim Yar Khan to visit her family. We then exchanged stories about our children's appetites (or lack thereof). Over time, shared tea led to a certain form of intimacy (or perhaps it was the late-night darkness outside or the sense of being the only women on the bus at that point). Over the next few hours, as we sat together, she shared her sorrow over her sister's recent death during childbirth and her own unmet desires for schooling. I recalled how carrying my sleeping children would sometimes lead to a dull ache in my arms and offered to hold her daughter so that Yasmeen could rest—and she happily handed her over. By now, it was three in the morning, but despite fatigue, I felt cosily cocooned by her presence and the domesticity of our interaction. A little later (with her daughter's little feet in my lap), I flipped through the letter section of a digest entitled *A Gathering of Sisters* and began reading.

Mussarat from Malakand Agency's concern for her children, Misbah from Karachi's sorrow over her nephew's death, and Shagufta from Alipur's high blood-pressure problems—the sharing in these letters sounded similar to Yasmeen from Rahim Yar Khan's sense of sorrow, 'Aunty' from Faisalabad's concern about her mother, and the young woman from Chowk Bahadur Shah's excitement at the family wedding, all of whom, in some way, I had met on this bus ride. Private sharing in public letters had always puzzled me but after this journey, these little windows into the readers' lives began to appear as a shared world of concern and connection that is public yet private, very similar to that which emerged here in the public space of a bus.

The interaction with Yasmeen was predicated on shared spatiality of a bus and a long journey. In contrast, the interaction with Simran and Kulsoom had no spatiality; the conversations were over the phone. Yet the shared details of domesticity, feelings about relationships, led to an emergence of trust that cut across our ethnic otherness.

I began realising that my conversations with Simran and Kulsoom had all been about the 'inner': family, domesticity, and relationships. We had rarely discussed the 'outer': political instability, violence. Yet the cocoon of our phone conversations had also blurred the rough edges of the outer and otherness for me. Somehow, the sphere of armed dacoits and kidnappings seemed to be held at bay because of the zone of connection formed by our conversations. Ethnic stereotypes of Sindhis as 'backward and non-modern' people who 'oppress' their women were overturned. In this time of ethnic and sectarian strife, the comfort zone of domesticity and everydayness with Yasmeen and with the writers from Sindh arose simultaneously and cut across ethnic and sectarian otherness. In other words, both with Yasmeen and with the writers from Sindh, the private had changed the public too. With Yasmeen, the domesticity of the conversation changed the alienating, all-male-passenger bus to a place of comfort. In the writers' case, our conversations about the everyday and the trivial had painted the outside in the same colours. The colours that shimmered through in their tone and voice as they shared the lively everydayness of their private lives had also organically spread over to the ethnic otherness of the outer and public.

This relates to the larger anthropological question of how we can look at others (and ourselves) and see what we did not see before. The question itself privileges sight and proximity (hence, 'look'). However, in this case, it was only hearing and listening that created new avenues for 'seeing' them and rural Sindh in ways that overcame otherness and created new ways of relating to one another.

DIGESTS IN A FAMILY OF SAINTLY STORYTELLERS

The monthly digests arrived during the same week as I did. There was a sense of excitement, almost festivity, as several young girls sat on the double bed and passed them to each other.

'Samina *api*'s story is in this—a novel.'

'No, this is Samina Ali, not Samina Azad.'

Twenty-year-old Laiba (fictitious name) possessively held one as her other cousins teased her about the time she sent a maid to get a digest and asked her to look for it under the pillow, where she knew the other cousin had hidden it. One of the older women turned to me. 'I had to ask for a double copy of each because otherwise I would just never get around to reading it.' With four digests and over sixteen women and girls who wanted to read them (and read them first), her comment was understandable. Later that night, as I got up to get some water, I saw Fauzia (fictitious name) hunched up on the next bed, reading with her phone's flashlight after a long day of taking care of the family's needs.

Fauzia, Laiba, and the other young girls live in a small village of about 1,500 to 2,000 people, located in Sindh. The village does not have a proper school, clinic, or even a large market. However, it is a short distance away from two major cities. Thus, physical access to these facilities is not difficult. They belong to a Syed family. Syeds are divided into several clans, such as Rajputs, Kazmis, and Makhdooms. Theirs is called Jillani through their lineage to Shah Abdul Qadir Jillani, a highly respected Sufi saint. Their direct ancestor was renowned for his generosity and hence came to be known as Sakhi (the generous one). He saw the accumulation of wealth and exploitation of devotees, commonly called *mureedeen*, as a sin. Thus, the family has a very simple lifestyle, and most of their men work for a salary. This is in contrast to the usual practice among religious guides, called *pirs*, of entering politics or depending upon monetary compensation for providing spiritual services.

Most Jillani Syeds (particularly in urban settings) have flexible rules regarding purdah or veiling. However, their family conventions are relatively strict. Women's mobility is restricted to mosques, shrines, relatives' houses, and visits to the doctor. 'We leave the house only for emotional healing or physical healing,' said one woman. The men of the family, non-purdah-observing friends or followers (*mureedeen*), help with shopping for clothes and other everyday requirements. If it's something significant which they want to select for themselves (for instance, curtains for a room), they remain in the car while the men of the family bring samples to show them. In addition, some of the older women also occasionally travel for pilgrimage (Hajj or Umrah) to Saudi Arabia.

None of the women have ever been to school. This is not because they are not permitted literacy. Currently, that's neither encouraged nor discouraged, but compromising the family prestige in terms of its women being publicly seen by unrelated men is a deal breaker. The boys of the family attend the school in the nearby city, but women's visibility (even veiled) compromises the family's reputation as practicing Syeds. In other words, even though their faces are hidden, the men are known in the city. Thus, when they accompany them, others can recognise them as the women of a particular family. However, even though unschooled, most of the girls know how to read Urdu, as well as their mother tongue, Sindhi. Two generations ago a teacher was posted to the village, and she was invited to live with the family, so a few of the girls began to study with her. She was only able to spend limited time, but Madare Shah (fictitious name), who is now in her fifties, learnt the Urdu and Sindhi script from her during that time.

MADARE SHAH: AGENCY AS A DECLARATION OF INDEPENDENCE

Like other members of the family, Madare Shah has several different names. Everyone commonly refers to her as *apa* (kin term for elder sister). However, she prefers Madare Shah (mother of Shah), a name she acquired when she adopted her nephew.

She is the eldest of five siblings (four sisters and a brother) and was adopted by her paternal uncle during infancy. Given the joint family system, she grew up with her siblings in the same house, but her paternal uncle made decisions about her education and financial independence. 'He had been living in Karachi for a long time, so his thinking was different from other people here,' she explained as we sat on her swing. It was her paternal uncle who arranged for the teacher to live in the house with them and teach the girls. That was not easy because at that time girls' education was regarded as breaking away from familial norms. Surprisingly, the strongest resistance came from another woman, his sister, who viewed it as defying norms prescribed for them by the elders. That notwithstanding, he persisted, and Madare Shah, along with another cousin, began to learn from her.

Two years later, the teacher was posted out of the village but by then, they had learned basic reading and writing. As she grew older, she expressed her desire to read monthlies, and her uncle asked a shopkeeper in the nearby city to keep one issue for the family. 'I was very pampered [*laadli*]—he never refused me anything,' she

Kinship chart

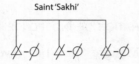

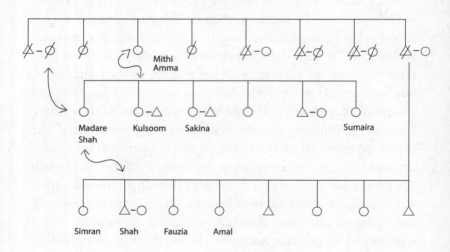

shared with a bright smile. I could easily believe that, as there was a very endearing childishness about her.

Madare Shah began by recording tales of kings and queens the elders narrated to her. As she grew older, around 1985, she began to write for several digests, such as *Sachi Kahaniyan* and *Shuaa*. Her favourite series was 'Three Women, Three Stories' (*Teen aurtain teen kahaniyan*) because it dealt with true stories. Madare Shah was prolific in sending stories, but she had to be careful about remaining anonymous. She never used her own name but the pen-names of *Shaam-e-gul-e-Tabassum* (the evening flower's smile), SB Jillani, or Ihtisham.

Madare Shah wrote for both weeklies and Sindhi newspapers, and she maintained that her stories were 'not lies, but based on truth—incidents I had heard about from our *mureedeen* or seen myself'.

One specific incident that compelled her to write was of a *mureed* in Thatta who had drowned at sea. Having abandoned the search for his body, his family was preparing to perform his last rites. They even had his *soyem* (the third day of ritual mourning and prayers for the deceased). Then, he arrived home, alive and well. 'Everyone was amazed: "What is this—how can this be? A lake is large enough, and then you have the river, but a sea? How could he survive in the sea?",' she related in her characteristic animated manner. 'He said, "When I fell off, I began to call out to my *pir*, and a boat arrived. The men threw a rope toward me, and, chanting Allah o Akbar [God is great], they pulled me back." So I wrote about that.' Turning around, she confirmed the name with her sisters and told me he was still alive.

One of her stories that led to some trouble was about a man who had shot his sister and then tried to kill himself. He died, but his sister survived. She however was paralysed for life because the bullet had pierced her back. The man's wife, who had been trying to save them both, was also hit by a bullet and died with her unborn baby. The doctor who treated this family was a friend of Madare Shah's cousins and shared this tale with them. She was deeply affected by it and wrote about the incident. Once the story was published, family members of the deceased began inquiring about who had written the story, but never really found out. 'Kiran, the digest editors had changed the last line and added, "Now there is a lion who lives and guards that house". But I was angry with them—why add this lie to something that is true?'

At the time, there was no payment for stories, but the digests would occasionally give awards and cash prizes. She won a cash prize award but could not receive it, partly because of purdah and partly because she did not want people to know she was writing. Writers are required to provide a return address and a contact number. Instead of her residential address, Madare Shah used the shopkeeper's address who got the digests for them; and in this way, her identity remained confidential.

These were the first two stories Madare Shah shared with me, but the first ones she actually wrote were about the effects of djinns (hidden mystical creatures created from smokeless fire which are mentioned in the Quran). She would regularly see women who were brought to their family for spiritual treatment, as they were perceived to be afflicted by djinns, and therefore her first stories were about them. As Madare Shah shared, 'I'd seen that a woman who was influenced would immediately untie her hair; even if it was tied in a braid, she would want it untied. I would ask them [the djinn inside the woman] their names and ask them to recite the first *kalima* [the verse that identifies you as a Muslim]. If they were Muslim djinns, they would. The voice, even the tone, would be that of a man, and I would try to treat them by holding the woman's little finger and reciting Quranic verses.'

A specific case Madare Shah witnessed and wrote about was of a young girl who helped around the house. The djinn would sometimes change shape and arrive at the door in the form of a Pakhtun or some other man, and it would be very difficult to prevent her from going to the door. She was under the djinn's influence for almost a year and a half, and during that time, Madare Shah would often see dirt, little stones, or filth coming out of her mouth. These effects were common to other people too, and Madare Shah began to tell me about a village where people were collectively afflicted by djinns. 'The village is not very far from here, and the Syed who heads it is now an MNA [Member of National Assembly].' She shared his name and related that a long time ago the entire village was experiencing problems. Crops would rot, stones would be thrown into people's houses, and they would see filth and dirt rather than cooked food. They enlisted the help of many Islamic scholars and spiritual leaders, but nothing seemed to work. They then approached Madare Shah's paternal grandfather, who recited Quranic verses, and the djinns finally left the village.

As Madare Shah shared her stories, it appeared as if digests became a private space, a metaphorical secret garden for her. No one in the family was aware that she was writing because none of them, apart from her sisters, was interested in reading digests. As she mentioned this, Madare Shah looked at her younger sister Sakina *apiya* (fictitious name) and began laughing. 'Kiran, she copied me and began to use the name of *Aab-e-gul Tabassum* [the flower nectar's smile]. She didn't write stories, but she would make me write letters for her which she would then send as hers.'

'Only once; just one letter,' Sakina added, and also began laughing.

Sakina *apiya* was an avid reader but she never wrote any stories because she felt her written Urdu was poor. Madare Shah had received tutoring but Sakina had learnt the Urdu script through the *Noorani Qaida,* a beginner's book of phonics for the Arabic script. The alphabets are somewhat similar, so she began to read Urdu while receiving Quranic education from her aunt, called *Jee jee ustad.* When I remarked how fluent her Urdu was, she began smiling. 'Tell that to my children; they always make fun of my Urdu. See, I could read because I was in the habit of reading digests out loud, and if my uncle was around, he would help me if I read a word wrong.' In addition, they had *mureedeen* in different parts of Pakistan with whom she had to communicate in Urdu.

I wondered what kind of stories Sakina might have written and decided they would have been parodies or comical sketches of ordinary everyday events and television plays. She was famous for mimicking relatives as well as characters she saw on television. At the time they were not allowed to have a television at home but their maternal uncle had one at his house. Each week she would especially drop in to watch her favourite plays and would then mimic the actors she had seen. A Pakistani television play, *Dhoop Kinaray*, about doctors, was her favourite. 'You remember that scene where Dr Sheena is ill and wants the hero's attention? I would perform the entire scene, mimicking them both.'

Her ability to find humour in everyday situations was apparent even now. As her husband spoke to me about his life and said 'When I married her,' she began laughing and quipped, 'What do you mean, "when I married *her*"—how many others did you marry before me?'

Sakina continued reading digests, often staying up nights so she could read stories. However, Madare Shah stopped writing after her uncle's death because she felt too depressed. She then adopted her nephew, and her life became extremely busy, so she no longer had the time to write. 'But I was the *pehli seerhi*' (first rung of the ladder), she added with a degree of pride. Madare Shah was able to go against family norms but rather than aggression, her playfulness appeared to be her strength. For instance, as we sat together, one of her nieces began telling me about their recent trip to Karachi with her son and daughter-in-law. They were supposed to visit a doctor whose clinic was near Sea View, a recreational area near the beach. When Madare Shah saw the rides, she insisted that she wanted to go on them. Her son was mortified, as it is regarded unseemly to make yourself visible to strange men. However, without giving him an opportunity to react, she happily went on various rides, including the roller-coaster.

'I was holding on to her tightly; I was so scared she would fall out,' she said, turning to Madare Shah, who was laughing with her. 'Remember how you would raise your arms and shout "Allah O Akbar"?' I find this significant because, during long car rides with the family, I had often witnessed arguments when women wanted to take off their face veils and men wanted them to wait till it was dark. The women continually complained but were generally obliged to give in. In contrast, through her playfulness, Madare Shah had done what she wanted to do (in major as well as minor matters, such as this one) and apparently managed it without any friction. In the incident shared here, she was the first in the family to read digests, the first to write for them, and the only one (as far as I could tell) who could push the boundaries of familial norms relating to propriety for women. Yet the usual connotations we associate with resistance, such as anger and bitterness, were absent. There was a kind of childish playfulness; a trust that others would understand and cooperate with her. It could be argued that she was in her fifties and could therefore push certain boundaries. However, there were other women in the family around her age who were unable to do so. For instance, I had witnessed Simran's mother arguing with her sons as we went on a five-hour car ride to her sister's village. She wanted to take off the face veil but they insisted that she keep it on till it was dark and no one could see inside the car. She displayed her annoyance and grumbled loudly for a long time, reminding her sons of how they had taken after their paternal family's unseemly traits. Her sons listened respectfully, occasionally trying to soothe her, but she had to keep it on. In this context, Madare Shah's gesture stands out as one of defiance which was not really through anger but playfulness and a faith in other people's ability to understand—she never asked her son, assuming all would be well, and it was.

Kulsoom: Agency as Social Work

Although Madare Shah was the 'first rung of the ladder' in terms of access to digests and writing for them, it was her younger sister Kulsoom (fictitious name) who took it up in earnest. She never received any tutoring in Urdu or Sindhi but learnt to read and write from digests that would regularly arrive at home. Kulsoom's aunt, commonly called Mithi amma (sweet mother), adopted her, so she grew up in her portion of the house.

Given her capacity for self-reflection, I asked her about the events in her childhood which she considered formative. She began by speaking about her aunt, Jee jee ustad, who had influenced her deeply; and how much she enjoyed all sports: rugby, biking, football, and especially cricket. However, the event that she saw as most crucial in shaping her was the demolition of Babri Mosque in India, when she was 14 years old.

> I was sitting outside on the swing. There was no power that day, and I heard on the radio that Babri Mosque had been martyred. It was as if my heart sank and time stopped [*jaisay dil baith jaata hai aur waqt thum jaata hai*]. I wanted to do something, and on that day, something changed in me.

Till that point she had been an avid listener of songs aired on All-India Radio, but after this incident, she gave that up. A few days later, one of her cousins brought an Indian movie. As they all sat down to watch it, Kulsoom got up and went to the storage room (*do chathi*) where her great-grandfather's books on Sufism (*Tasawuff*) were kept and took to reading them.

I asked her if she had wanted others to join her, just as they wanted her to join them in watching the movie. 'I always wanted to be gifted a book, but no one ever did.' She laughed. 'My cousins would say, "You can read a book only once, so why shouldn't we buy you a lipstick which can be used over and over again?".'

Through extensive digest reading, Kulsoom could fluently read Urdu, so she was able to understand the relatively difficult language religious books utilised. In addition, she began noting down the names of literary books or books on religion which were reviewed in these monthlies. She would then give the list to her cousin (Madare Shah's son, who is now her husband). He studied in the nearby city and would borrow them from the library. He was on friendly relations with the library staff, so he enjoyed going there, but this often posed a problem when he reached home long after the college had closed. Nonetheless, she had access to new reading material of her choice as the library staff also began purchasing the books she recommended.

In response to my question about what prompted her to write in digests, she said that she was primarily interested in the lives of Sufi saints (*buzurg*, respected people). 'I used to read these books, and I would wonder, "How did these people become the way they are?" I would read of their struggle [*jang*] with self [*nafs*], such as not eating an apple for thirty years because they wanted to understand and overcome the desire for it. So I began to feel that worldly aspects are shallow or insignificant [*duniya ki saari cheezain suthai hain*].'

She paused and then related two narratives that had a great effect on her. I'm writing the summary here, but her style was that of religious books where narration is in a loop.

1. The Prophet Noah had to collect not only animals but also plants. He realised that he was missing grapevine. Satan [*shaitan*] had stolen it, so he went to ask him for it. The devil replied, 'You can have it back, but I will water it'." He then watered it first with jackal's blood, then pig's, and then a lion's. These represent the three stages of being intoxicated: first you become as scared as a jackal, then you become as lustful as a pig, and the last stage is that you become fearless, like a lion. Thus, alcohol is forbidden in Islam because it can take you away from your humanness and reduce you to an animal.

2. After Adam and Eve were sent out to Earth, Satan took his son, *khannas* [literally, the one who hides after appearing], and brought him to Eve. She was alone at home, and he pressured her to keep him. She protested, but he didn't listen. Then when Adam came home, he got angry and drowned *khannas* in water. When Satan learnt of this, he shouted for

him to come out, and he jumped out of the water. The same thing happened when Adam put it into fire. The third day, Adam slaughtered it, and both he and his wife ate it. Satan was very happy because this is what he wanted all along, as now *khannas* was a part of both of them. So now *khannas* is a part of our being [*ab humaray undar baitha hua hai*] and makes us scared and anxious through fearful thoughts that have no real basis [*vasvasay*]. This is why we were given the Quranic verses of Surah al-Nas.

This interweaving of the everyday with a spiritual outlook was also apparent in little things. For instance, as she complained about her toddler, who loved to eat mud, she added, 'We've come from dust, so this is why, as humans, we're still drawn to it'.

Aside from communicating what she understood of the world through this outlook, her primary motivation for writing was to 'do something'. As we cleaned prawns for lunch, she continued; given their familial norms, she could not be a social worker or a lawyer. The only real possibility then was to become a writer. After obtaining her brother's permission, she began to think of pen-names. She thought of several different ones but couldn't decide. Then one day, as she sat at a religious gathering (*Milad*), she began crying. 'You know how you are sometimes moved to tears because of the mood [*kaifiath*] you are in at these gatherings? I sat with my head on my knees so no one would see me weeping. That's when my pen-name came to my mind: "the servant".'

This name also seemed appropriate to her because in this way, her 'pen would not sway' (*qalam behkay ga nahin*)'. She felt that writers often forget that their work has a real effect on people. From their perspective, they highlight the negativity so it can be addressed but in reality, those with weak minds are negatively influenced. She gave the example of a politician in Larkana who had been killed by his brother. The family later recounted how the murderer had read a story in a digest about disposing of a body by burning it. Thus, although he already had the inclination, the method was pointed out through a fictional account.

Kulsoom's first story was on spirituality and revolved around a man who becomes a 'spiritual vagabond' (*malang*) after the woman he loved passed away. She had also translated Sindhi verses by the Sufi saint Shah Abdul Latif Bhittai (1689–1752) to depict how the loss or lack of love is often the greatest loss. 'This is not just in terms of romantic love; even a child who feels unloved or insufficiently loved by parents experiences this pain that is often responsible for failures in life.' She pointed out that portraying this in Urdu was not easy, as there are countless words (and shades of meaning) for love in Sindhi, but only five in Urdu (*ishq, mohabbat, pyaar, chahat,* and *uns*).

Her first story was not published, partly because it was late and partly because it was seen as too heavy for digest audiences. Nonetheless, the editor gave encouraging feedback and urged her to keep writing. Kulsoom's second story (published in January 2004) was about honour killings. Women who visited them had told her of a graveyard where fifteen women were killed and buried as *kari* (someone who has been accused of and killed for maintaining illicit relations) without any of the burial rituals. 'I knew that this is not allowed in Islam; you cannot kill anyone, not even a woman who is proven to be *kari*, and here there were fifteen who were killed on the basis of suspicion.'

Kulsoom wove her story around a man who finds his wife in a sugarcane field. Noticing my puzzled expression, she explained, 'See, in villages, there are no casinos or restaurants but sugarcane fields are tall and provide shelter [*panahgaah*] because no one can see once you're inside.' He finds her with another man and kills her. He is then sentenced and spends seven years in jail (the law at the time; now it has changed to the death sentence, she clarified). As he comes out, he's surprised to see no one from his family is there to receive him. When he reaches home, he discovers that his cousin has been accused as *kari*. The only way a woman's life can be saved in these cases is if a man offers to marry her. This is what he does because, during his stay in jail, he realised that what he did was both morally and religiously wrong, and wants to correct that.

Similarly, her short story entitled 'Naqsh i qadam' (following; literally, following footsteps) was also drawn from a sense of correcting what she saw around her.

> I would see people around me calling a man who listens to his wife or follows her advice by derogatory words like *zunn mureed* (excessively fond of, or submissive to, a wife). It, however, occurred to me that every man who goes for Hajj has to follow in Bibi Hajra's footsteps.
>
> So when I thought of this, I wrote a story about a man who is always anxious about not being seen as subservient to his wife but when he goes for Hajj, he realises that he does not have a choice—he has to follow in a woman's footsteps.

Some of her stories, such as that entitled 'Abortion' (changed to 'Motherhood' by the editor), are based on real incidents. One of the women who helped around the house told her about coming across a newborn baby in the fields. She wanted to save the baby but changed her mind when she thought that people might think it was her daughter's illegitimate child because she had been ill for a few months. The following day, when she went back, she saw its mutilated body; animals had killed it during the night. 'I told her, "You could have brought the baby to us; we could have given it to a childless couple among our *mureedee*". I also thought of setting up a centre like the Edhi welfare centre where people can leave unwanted babies, but for practical initiatives, you need resources, and resources can only be acquired if you have freedom [of mobility].'

New Identities

Whereas Madare Shah's pen-name was primarily a source of anonymity, in Kulsoom's case it has become an avenue towards a new identity. She has given both her daughters similar names. The name we give a child is always reflective of our values and inclinations but in her family, names have an additional significance. Most of the teenaged cousins are named after elders who have passed away. Moreover, each child usually has another name given by an aunt or uncle. When Kulsoom was asked to name her younger cousin, she did so after the digest editor who had honed her writing skills. Thus, in naming her daughters as well as her cousin, Kulsoom went against familial norms and privileged her pen-name and her association with digests.

'What would you have been, if you had not become a writer?' I asked.

'Social worker,' she replied without a moment's hesitation. To me she seemed to be both, a writer as well as a social worker. Her organisational skills and an ability to nurture those around her were visible in several ways. During the day I would see her tending not only to her own little children and husband, but also Mithi amma, her biological mother, as well as an elderly uncle who was unable to speak. Giving meals, ensuring that they had appropriate clothing for the weather, and keeping their things in order, were all a regular part of her day. Thus, the gesture her uncle used to refer to her: tapping his chest to signify 'mine' (the one who takes care of me).

This sense of nurturing also extends beyond the familial circle to the village. In this context, she has taken several initiatives. One of the first steps was establishing a library where women could borrow books. She also set up a rotation system to ensure that they would actually read some of the more challenging texts. Each member also had to give a weekly report on a book, which was then discussed and debated.

Similarly, during the floods, as people poured into their home to find shelter, she used her contacts with other writers and arranged for temporary camps and food. I could see how the writers trusted her with their charity. When I mentioned that my sister wanted to contribute, she gave me a tabulated account of the homes in the village which did not have direct access to water (there are only a few tube wells in the village) and how one could distribute it geographically, as well as the different materials that would be required and their cost breakdown.

One morning, as I played with her daughters, I asked her what she wanted for their future. To my surprise, rather than a profession (writer, lawyer, social worker) as I imagined she would say, she quietly began telling me how she wanted them both to become *aalima* and *fazila* (someone who is well versed in religious studies). Her practical efforts also indicate this choice. One day, I heard her arguing with her husband about her elder daughter's schooling, as she was now over five years old. Her husband did not have a problem with her education. He however pointed out that the school was in the nearby city (forty minutes away), so they would have to arrange for someone to pick her up and drop her back as his own work hours were quite late. Given her young age, they needed someone responsible; and therefore schooling at this point was simply not possible.

In our conversations too, Kulsoom would often express her concern about her children not having a regular structure to their day. She had often tried to establish a routine for them but given the joint family system, this was not always possible. Yet, notwithstanding all these practical difficulties, Kulsoom seems to have found a way out by establishing a madrassa/school for girls on the second floor of the portion of the house they are currently building to enable her daughters, along with other children, to have a regular routine. Her attention to detail came to the fore again when she asked me to check the process for madrassa or school registration so she could get the paperwork completed while the physical infrastructure was being constructed.

Kulsoom's efforts for her daughters' future have yet to materialise. However, she has already paved the way for her younger cousins, such as Simran, who has not only continued digest writing but is now also writing scripts for television.

Simran: Agency as Authenticity

Simran (whom we met in the first chapter) is the eldest of seven siblings and was adopted by Madare Shah when she was an infant. However, when her younger brother was born, he was adopted by Madare Shah, and she went back to her parents. 'You gave me back; you thought, "He's a boy—he'll take better care of me" but see how I take care of you, and he's useless,' she teased Madare Shah as she told me this.

Simran was often ill as a child; this proved to be a blessing in disguise as she was spared the housework that her other sisters had to undertake. Therefore she had more time for writing and thinking than her younger sisters, Fauzia, Nosheen, and Amal (fictitious names). More than her health, it was her father's support that paved the way for numerous options. 'My father gave me *izzat* [respect] as well as *mohabbat* [love]. In many ways I could do as I pleased; like, we are not supposed to leave the house, but as a teenager I would often accompany my father when he travelled.'

She has had no formal schooling but was helped and guided by Kulsoom. However, their attitudes toward digest writing are very different. For Kulsoom, stories are predominantly about social messages. In contrast, Simran sees fiction as something that has a life of its own.

> When sorrow or deprivation [*mehroomi*] turn in their slumber [*mehroomi ya dukh jo karvat laita hai*], that's what makes you write. Anyone can write a story, but you have to enter within yourself.

It's both very difficult and very easy; feelings travel through that [from the writer to the reader]. If you mess with your story [treat it with disrespect or inauthentically], the story will also mess with you [*agar aap kahani ke saath mazaq karainge kahani bhi aap ke saath mazaq karegi*].

Rather than a linear narrative as such, her stories often revolve around states of mind or moods. The first story she shared with me was about a woman who used to write fiction but is now caught up in domestic responsibilities.

The characters say, 'You were our mother, but you've abandoned us', and she says, 'What can I do? I have to wash clothes, make breakfast, and I'm too tired. I can't be with you anymore'. She feels guilty and sad, but while the characters are conveying their hurt, she falls asleep as a consequence of the exhaustion of daily toil.

Her first attempt at writing fiction was around the age of fourteen or fifteen, with a short story. She did not send it to be published or even show it to Kulsoom because she felt she would point out too many holes in it (*itnay keerhay nikalainge*). Earlier, she had been writing short, comical verses and sending them to children's magazines. She partly ascribed her wish to write as something that was drawn from the people around her. Kulsoom had begun writing; Madare Shah would read and have a lot of books in her room; and her father would also bring her books. Above all, however, she sees this creativity as arising from the familial customs (*mahol*) that did not allow a routine or a life outside. 'The more you bound a person, the more that person turns inwards. As the outside is eliminated, we turn within.'

Some of her short stories were inspired by the people to whom she was drawn. For instance, one of her short stories was initially written as a page in her diary which she wrote after a close friend's unexpected death. She shared that while she was writing it, it appeared to her that her friend's writing style was coming though in her own work. 'Sentences such as, "Like the second hand of the clock, you never stop ticking in my heart", or "Which one do you think is the longest hand of the clock: love or death?"—these were lines that my friend might have written, but not me.'

Another short story was written after the 2010 floods. 'There was a risk that our area might be inundated. So I began to worry about my books and what would happen if I were to lose them. When I realised how deep that fear was, I began to think of people who had lost books they loved and based a story on that.'

Her favourite work, and the one she most discussed with me, is her novel: 'This is a story that the characters made me write at gunpoint.' Laughing, 'Sometimes I would be in their grip, and sometimes they would be in mine.'

The story revolves around a sixty-year-old man called Funkaar (artist). He's been painting and writing and has had to face criticism by people who see these activities as un-Islamic.

> I had a lot of questions, like, why do we write stories? Is it wrong to write fiction? But there comes a point when you go beyond good and bad, and that's when you find out how beneficent Allah can be [*Allah ki rehmat ka andaza ho jaata hai*]. So the main idea was a kind of messiness [*betarteebi*] and rebellion. There wasn't really a plot as such but just this character. Funkaar had experienced love; he had experienced fulfilment through work; now he wondered what he had left to live for. And this was my question too. After you are married and you've raised a family, around the age of sixty, is there just loneliness and death, or could there be something else? I think this is also the fear that gets people to look for temporary support [*aarzi saharay*].

Initially, she was afraid of exploring this idea because she felt fearful about what it might lead to. 'Many scorpions might come out, and it will be painful, the same way you don't want to enter a dark alley.' However, when a digest editor asked her to contribute something, Simran did not want to say no outright, so she offered to write a novel rather than a short story. It is relatively difficult to make space for a novel, so she assumed the digest editor would not ask her again. However, she contacted her again to tell her that they had made space in the next few issues, and Simran should begin writing her novel.

> To write something long, you need something that is either in your grip or you're in its grip. After the first episode, the story wrote itself. [Pausing] Stories always write themselves. But one has to wait for the story to have enough energy. Like, when I have to send an episode, I keep writing, whether it's day, night, morning, or evening. Just like you have to step outside to gaze at the sky; similarly, with this story it's like entering a well, and often I am surprised at what the characters make me write.

In this context she shared a specific example. In the first episode, Funkaar boards a train and meets a fellow passenger, Kabeer, who predicts that Funkaar will die in eight months and eight days because Kabeer can see death in his eyes. When Simran wrote these lines in the first episode, she had planned on ending Funkaar's character toward the eighth episode. However, when she reached that stage, it had too many subplots and could not be ended.

> I then found myself writing a dialogue for Ali Gohar [another character] that the person who is approaching death sees it in everyone's eyes around him. That way, I found the answer and ended Kabeer's character instead. We tend to see our own feelings in another person's eyes but this didn't become clear till I wrote this.

CONTEXTUALISING AGENCY

Let us now contextualise these three writers' trajectories by expanding on some key strands of the discussion. At one level, these women are modern-day 'secluded scholars'. The historian Gail

Minault (1998) uses this term for South Asian women writers in the eighteenth and nineteenth centuries who learnt to read and write in the face of overwhelming odds. Thus, just like Ashrafunnisa Begum (1998: 26), who learnt the Urdu script by copying it with coal left in the kitchen, these writers are extraordinary in their creative capacity and resilience. Literacy and mobility, often taken for granted in mainstream situations, were not available to them, yet they have succeeded in achieving both. Although their bodies continue to reside within a limited sphere, they have been able to mobilise their voices through digest fiction, and these voices now circulate in unknown spheres, both literal and metaphorical.

We tend to see agency and resistance as overcoming class, socio-economic, or other structural obstacles an individual might face; a kind of going against all odds that leads to a fundamental change in circumstances. In other words, the usual connotations of agency include an individual being able to overcome structural obstacles and create opportunities that seemed impossible or at least extremely unlikely in their particular context. In the case of these writers, the primary restrictions of mobility and education continue. In this sense, their circumstances have not changed, so the actualisation of possibilities (becoming an editor, social worker) remains within the realm of fiction. In this context, then, how do we position their agency?

Foucault's insights on power and Abu Lughod's reflections on resistance are relevant here because they allow us to go beyond the framework of agency being valid only when it overturns power structures. In *The History of Sexuality* (1990), Foucault, as is commonly understood, delineates between the terminal forms power takes, such as sovereignty of the state, form of law, and overall domination, and its strategies as the multiplicity of force relations (Foucault, 1990: 92). More important for our purposes, he highlights that 'power is accompanied with resistance, so one is always "inside" power; there is no "escaping" it' (1980: 95). Abu Lughod builds on this Foucauldian notion of power and its entanglement with resistance. She suggests that romanticising resistance as a sign of the ineffectiveness of power structures and the freedom of the human spirit leads to two problems. First, focusing on abstract theories of power and agency without taking into account their complex entanglement denies us insights that a methodological focus on power and its accompanying resistance within a specific context can yield about the techniques of power and its changing forms. Second, and particularly relevant for our purpose here, the measure of success or authenticity of resistance becomes tied up in how well it overturns oppositional power structures. Thus, the relationship between power and agency in this context is one of entanglement rather than overturning.

Madare Shah, Kulsoom, and Simran are three very different writers. Even the way they communicated their stories greatly varied. For instance, Kulsoom's narrative carried a linear progression in terms of which story she wrote first, what the characters were about, and what message she wished to convey. Therefore, although Kulsoom was unable to become a social worker, she has been able to convey social messages through her fiction, which she also sees as a form of social work. In contrast, Simran's narrative had no clear beginning or end. To give a concrete example regarding their writing processes, Kulsoom has a diary with ideas for stories she wants to write. Each story has an outline with key words such as 'Income support programme, problems women encounter, main character an old woman based in Thatta'. In contrast, Simran's ideas are flows that she experiences and writes about: a certain state of mind, a certain mood, which are then grafted on to a character. For Simran, stories are about exploration, going down a path where the end is neither visible nor certain. Madare Shah, on the other hand, emphasised the truth of her stories, in that each of the incidents was real: something that happened to her or something that she had witnessed.

In other words, how each sees the process of fiction writing varies, yet the motivation appears to be similar. There is what Abu

Lughod (1999) in her research on Bedouin poetry terms 'veiled sentiments': feelings that do not enter daily discourse but can be safely articulated through creative expression. In a sense, this is a way of resisting daily realities without posing a fundamental challenge to the system itself. In the case of these three writers, it takes the form of writing about unmet desires (such as romance) as well as vicariously living lives that are not really possible in their own context (employment, social work, university life).

To take an example, a few months earlier, the editor of a Sindhi magazine had offered Simran a job. They had had several conversations about Sindhi literature. Given her grasp of the subject, he had assumed she had a Master's in Sindhi. He therefore offered her an editorial position and asked her to bring her degrees so it could be finalised. Because of her lack of formal education, Simran was unable to pursue this option. However, she has been able to experience it vicariously through one of her characters, a young girl named Amrit. Her vivid descriptions of how Amrit organises her workload are all, in a sense, projections of desires for possibilities that are impossible yet graspable through imagination. Thus, through the fictional character of Amrit, Simran is able to experience the sense of having a career and the daily toil of formal employment. Kulsoom, on the other hand, has managed to alter digest writing itself into a form of social work by incorporating messages in her stories which she wishes to communicate. However, at another level, this can also be viewed as a search for authenticity, both for themselves and their experiences, which has assumed different forms in each case.

BEYOND THE BOUNDS OF RATIONALITY

When Madare Shah, the 'first rung of the ladder', began writing, it was directed to an audience which was unaware of her family status. Becoming Sham-e-gul-e-Tabassum, a name that lacks the prefixes of Shah or Syeda which denote a certain religious status, allowed an identity that went beyond her status as a Syeda. In a sense, this was a declaration of independence and a stepping out. In this new sphere, prestige and acceptance had to be gained through the skill of writing stories that were good enough to be published and read. Her first stories were about the extraordinary events she witnessed because of her family's position as spiritual healers. Although she was going beyond family identity and norms by writing, the subjects on which she focused revolved around the position of her family: djinns that afflicted women, drowning men who were saved. In that context, her stories can be positioned as an attempt to not merely articulate emotions she could not openly share but also to decipher and authenticate her own experiences regarding spirituality which clash with mainstream notions on the boundaries of rationality. A generation later, Simran's writing carries the same element. For most digest readers, the world in which Simran lives or how she experiences it is often incomprehensible. For instance, the primary problem she had with her novel was attempting to frame spiritual experiences within a logical framework. In one of the initial episodes, she depicted a man who disappears; the editor pointed out that later she would have to explain his disappearance.

> But see, I didn't have an explanation. A few days before that, Baba [father] had gone to a shrine. On his way there, he met a person to whom he gave a ride. That person said, 'You're going because of two problems; the first one will be resolved now and the second three months from now'. Baba was surprised because he had not discussed these problems with anyone. Later, when they entered the shrine, the man was in front of them, but then when they looked up, he had simply disappeared, and no one had seen him leave.

During my stay in their village, some of my own assumptions about reality and belief systems were also overturned. Let me narrate one particular incident. Simran's father is severely diabetic and had an open sore that would not heal. One day, as we travelled to drop off Simran's mother at her maternal village, we stopped by a small hill. Simran and her siblings teased their mother about her Urdu as she explained to me that there was a stream on this hill which had healing properties. The Sufi saint Lal Shahbaz Qalandar (1149–1300) was initially supposed to be buried here but the site of his burial was later changed. When the hill heard of this, it exploded with grief, and the streams are the tears that it continues to shed.

We walked up the barren hill to a small pond of water where several people were bathing. There were clothes strewn on the side, as it is customary to leave old clothes there. To my eyes, the green water appeared contaminated; I saw several people with skin ailments bathing in it. I kept my concerns to myself but debated it inwardly, fearing that her father's open wound might get infected. My fears were unfounded; a few days later, Simran called me excitedly and showed the new skin which had begun growing over his wound. From one perspective, it is sulphur or other minerals in that water that help with healing, but from another point of view, it is the faith in its healing properties that led to this outcome. Whether you consider this water to be tears shed by the hill or contaminated, fungus-ridden liquid may determine your physical reaction. In this instance, I had seen for myself how rationality or the modern perspective of contamination was overturned. Had the water been used for me, it could surely have led to an infection but given Simran and her family's faith in it, the dynamic was very different for them. My point is that their bodies have restricted mobility but, given their position as faith healers and spiritual leaders, they often witness or undergo experiences that defy mainstream bounds of reality. Writing, for them, then becomes an avenue for both deciphering and describing these experiences.

Let me briefly turn to the feminist philosopher Elizabeth Grosz, as her reflections on the link between mind and body are relevant for our purpose here. She uses the metaphor for body as surface and mind as text, and highlights that all etchings have to take into account the surface on which they are being written. Thus, rather than a simple tabula rasa, bodies have their own dynamics and effects on works that are considered to be of the mind, such as writing, ideas, or art. Just as the material surface of a text introduces certain flows and inhibits others, the texture of the surface (body) affects the flow of calligraphic etching (works of the mind). There is an 'uncontrollable drift' of the body into the mind and of the mind into the body (Grosz, 1994: xii). Her argument is the context of sexually specific male and female bodies. However, in this case, we have bodies that experience the world from very particular vantage points and minds which then interpret these experiences and attempt to bring them into the mainstream discourse. The episode at the stream opened up notions of spiritual powers and healing but also brought up the issue of mobility.

FETTERED SPACES AND UNFETTERED TIME

I would often hear Simran, Kulsoom, and the rest of the cousins discussing lack of mobility through expressions such as 'We are like frogs in a well' (*hum koinh ke maindak hain*), 'We spend our childhood, our youth, and our old age within these walls' (*yaheen bachpan, yaheen jawani, yaheen burhapaa*)'. However, the restrictions in mobility truly hit home through two experiences.

One evening, Simran and I were sitting on the roof when her younger cousin, ten-year-old Abu Bakr, excitedly announced that a trip to the local mosque was being planned. We had to wait till it was dark, so we continued chatting and various cousins joined our conversation. Around 10 pm or so, we all went down to where the girls were getting ready. There was an air of festivity and playful arguments about who had lost whose veil as they got ready. Each draped herself in a burqa, then a veil (covering the face), and finally a dupatta.

Sakina, a village woman who helped with household chores, went around excitedly telling us who would be joining in and what stage of preparation the various girls were in. I asked Simran if I needed to cover my face too, as I usually accompanied them in a chador with my face visible. She began laughing and told me it was nearby. After almost forty minutes of preparation, we finally headed out as a group. Simran's male cousins, Abu Bakr, and his elder brother first checked outside to ensure there was no one nearby and then asked us to proceed. To my surprise, the mosque was literally three steps from the main door. Thus, all the preparation and care that had gone into getting ready for this trip seemed as pointless to me as polishing firewood.

Once we were inside the mosque, some of the girls began reciting religious poetry while others swept the prayer room. After a little while, as we headed back home, the girls began to insist that they go to the nearby shrine past the lake. The male cousins and older aunts were initially reluctant but eventually agreed, so we walked by the lake. The girls pretended to push each other into the water or giggled loudly as they ran after each other. Later, when we returned home, everyone congregated in our room, talking about the trip. During the conversation Simran asked her brother to show me the village railway station. It is a prominent feature in most of her stories. However, as they talked about it, I began realising that her last trip to the station had been when she was a child. Thus, whatever she writes now is from her memories of what it looked like. As she described some parts of it, her younger brother corrected her, saying that it was all gone now (*ab toh khandar bun gaya hai*), and she wondered aloud when she would be able to see it next.

Similarly, on another occasion, as I travelled with Simran, we stopped by a market. Her brothers went out to buy some food while we waited in the car. While we were waiting, we noticed that the nearby shop carried a dessert the girls liked. I headed out to get some and then remembered that Simran couldn't accompany me. These moments were often evocative of Aasia Djebar's autobiographical note in the novel *Fantasia* (1993).[1] In a particularly moving passage, she writes about visiting her cousins. Their mobility is restricted but they write letters that circulate in unknown spheres.

During these moments I was truly grateful for my mobility. However, these moments revealed far more complexity than a simplistic binary of mobility equals freedom and empowerment, while immobility equals restriction. Challenges also carry their own productive force. Let me make a slight detour, because the anthropologist Brian Larkin's insight is relevant to what I am suggesting here. In his ethnography on Nigerian cinema, Larkin (2008) highlights that the overarching paradigm of development positions disruptions as restrictive. However, apparently restrictive phenomena can also have a productive aspect. For instance, the regular breakdown of vehicles in Nigeria has led to a thriving industry of mechanics.

Similarly, the challenges Simran has had to face carry a productive force. Let me explain this through an example. As we dropped off Simran's mother at her ancestral village, we decided to stop by Sehvan Sharif, a famous Sufi saint's shrine. Simran, her brothers, little Shifa, and I took off our shoes and walked barefoot toward the brightly lit, dome-shaped building. As we passed through the open courtyard, we noticed a group of men who were dancing to a *dhol*.[2] This form of dance, called *dhamaal*, is usually regarded as spiritual. As we stood by watching them, I pointed out a man who seemed oblivious to his surroundings and danced with an abandon which was very captivating. I joked that it reminded me of the character Ali Gohar from her novel. This is a young man whose life revolves around the question of *deen aur duniya*, the tension between living in the world and attempting to connect to something beyond. This man's dance carried a shade of that abandonment. For me, this was an offhand remark but Simran seemed to ponder it seriously as she thought aloud, 'What would he be doing here? Why would he be dancing with such abandon?'

As we waited in the car while her brothers got us ice cream, Simran still seemed enamoured by what we had witnessed.

The next morning, as I told Kulsoom about our trip, Simran began to write. A few minutes later, Simran's blank page carried these lines:

How could he not crumble [*woh kaisay na barbaad hota*]? To experience fulfilment, he held passion's [*ishq*] hand and began wandering. When he got tired, he lay down on passion's doorstep [*ishq ke dar per*]. Upon waking up, he had lost himself; he was not there, he had left himself. He had abandoned himself to passion's flow [*ishq ke haal per*]. His state of mind was not his own [*Iss ki halath ghair thee*]. At times he would find himself dancing to passion's tune [*ishq ke isharon per nachta tha*], and at other times, passion would dance to his tune [*ishq us ke isharon per nachta tha*]. Passion had pampered him, spoiled him [*sar charha lia tha ishq ne*]. His being was full of joy, full of love [*daaman khushiyon se bhar gaya tha mohabbat se bhar gaya tha*].

She had articulated that man's state of mind as she perceived it and planned on adding these lines to Ali Gohar's character once she had figured out the why and how of his visit to Sehvan Sharif. My point is that although restrictions in mobility have led to lost opportunities, they have also led to an intensified gaze in engaging with the outside. The conversations about the trip to the mosque or the discussions on what might have been going on with the man we observed were forms of this engagement. Her gaze is intensified because there are fewer opportunities to engage with the outside. Her engagement with spaces (other than her home) is intermittent and infrequent. This in turn leads to a certain intensity of engagement which is otherwise usually not present.

Moreover, as I returned to Islamabad, although I appreciated the easy access I had in terms of mobility, I realised that while I may have the freedom of unrestricted spatial mobility, Simran has the freedom of unfettered time. My life is restricted through the pressure of deadlines and regulated chunks (picking up and dropping the children to school, interviewing, writing). There is a rush to move on, to undertake the next task, which leaves little room for contemplation; hence, my casual moving on when I saw that man. In contrast, although Simran has lost opportunities which formal education could have led to, the lack of formal schooling has also led to an organic development of her perspective and abilities. I have no doubt that she would have been exceptionally successful in any formal educational structure, yet I wonder whether her fiction would have remained as original and intense as it is now. I should also point out that there was an easy sense of connection, a playfulness, which ran contrary to the portrayal of purdah-observing women as depressed or passive.

In this context, challenges provide a possibility but it is a possibility that you may or may not pursue. Thus far I have related a linear story of engagement with digests and fiction as a search for self-expression and agency. However, as always, reality is far more complex. Madare Shah, Kulsoom, and Simran have used the medium of fiction but for some other women in the family, fiction is 'the world of lies'. The most intriguing case of disengagement is that of Kulsoom's younger sister Sumaira, who became a digest writer but then disengaged from fiction altogether.

SUMAIRA: AGENCY AS DISENGAGEMENT

Sumaira (fictitious name) began to learn to read at around the age of twelve or so, later than her cousins who could already read Sindhi. Their aunt, Jee jee ustad, asked Kulsoom to teach her, and she began taking lessons. Sumaira shared that she was not a keen learner, but Kulsoom's patience paid off. 'Sometimes I would not go to her for four days and would even wish that she would get angry with me or scold me, but she never did.'

Gradually, Sumaira became fluent in Quranic education as well as Sindhi and Urdu. Kulsoom then began to give her books related to fiction, even heavy reading such as Mumtaz Mufti's *Alakh Nagri*. Over time, she herself began writing and sharing her stories with Kulsoom for correction. Because Kulsoom had already paved the way in terms of getting their eldest brother to agree to let them write stories, there was no problem at home.

Over time Kulsoom, Sumaira, and Kulsoom's cousin Simran formed a small group. Each of them wrote stories and shared them with the other two. There was also a symbolic element with them gifting one other paper and pens as birthday presents.

Publishing did not always run smooth. Simran and Sumaira were both sending stories. The same mailing address, similar handwriting, and even the same paper led editors to believe that this was a single person attempting to get published by writing under two names. Once the confusion was cleared, Sumaira's stories began to be published and received favourable feedback. However, in 2011, she decided to stop writing and now has even given up reading digests.

'Sumaira had some dreams, so she got scared and doesn't write stories any more,' Madare Shah and Simran shared as we sat on the roof. I was intrigued by this but didn't get an opportunity to interact with her for several days. Other cousins would constantly trail in and out of each other's homes, but I never saw Sumaira, which further reinforced my impression of her as someone who had withdrawn and isolated herself.

One morning, during breakfast, I asked Simran to take me to Sumaira so I could speak to her about her stories. "Don't waste time changing; let's just go as we are. You can shower in Sumaira's bathroom; if we wait, someone will drop in.' I quickly grabbed my tape recorder, and we set off for the portion she shares with her mother. Aside from a colourful *ralli* (traditional Sindhi patchwork bedspread), her room seemed unadorned. The sonic world was, however, rich and vibrant; a rooster crowing in the background and various early morning voices enveloped us.

We sat chatting with her mother while we waited for Sumaira to emerge from the bathroom. Relatively tall, with large, expressive eyes, she seemed genuinely happy to see us.

All three of us sat on her bed with the tape-recorder between us as I explained that I wanted to learn more about her stories. I began by asking her about the story she liked most from her own work.

'I've forgotten it now (*ab toh bhool bhaal gaya*), but it's about this landlord [*vadera*] who tells his child that his mother ran away. Now, you know, children always side with their mother, so from the very beginning, this child thinks his mother was not to blame; she was innocent [*bayqasoor*]. So in response to people's questions he says, "I only know that my father was wrong, people were wrong; my mother was not to blame".'

'And what about the story you wrote about floods?' I prompted.

'It was the way they were displaced' (*durr durr ki thokrain khaaeen unhon ne*).

'Which year was this?' I asked.

Looking toward Simran, she confirmed, '2010?' and continued, 'About 200,000 people were affected. Those with a good reputation (*izzat*) lost their respectability. They had to beg from other people; cattle, land—it was all lost.'

Sumaira had seen these people herself because many of them had taken refuge in their home and in the story depicted their hopelessness:

The refugees' camp seemed to have a festival [mela] of sadness, misery, and rootlessness. In this festival, individual sadness was lost, as an abandoned child feels lost. This festival will continue for several days. No one knows what will happen. Everyone's eyes carry dreams of returning home, [these are] lost travellers who are uncertain of their future, of how many more indignities and humiliations fate has in store for them [*durr ki thokrain khana unn ka muqaddar hai*] ... The ones who had diverted this water had saved the stores that held sugar that was to be sold at prices much higher than what was needed. This sugar had been saved.[3]

The story's main character is a little girl who goes to camp to look for food. Sumaira's primary concern was to make it plain that floods were not a natural disaster, but caused by the government. Prominent politicians had diverted water away from their own sugar mills, thus flooding large areas of cultivated land. 'I had even written the names of the politicians, but they [editors] removed them.'

Kulsoom, who was her teacher, had always told her that 'Whatever you write has to have a good message; it should make a home for itself in people's hearts' *logon ke dilon main ghar kar jaaye*); thus, she tried each time to have a clear message in her stories.

When I asked her why she decided to stop writing, her first response was, 'I left it because I thought I'm not going to get anything from it. What is the point of such fame that I get without the name of *Rusullallah* [Prophet Muhammad (PBUH)]?'

'How come?' I asked, puzzled by her response.

'I am going to write. I don't have any material, but I am going to write. I want to write about *ahadith*, I want to write about the glory [*shaan*] of the one who gives us everything. Life starts and ends with that—what else is there? My mother also used to tell me, "Sumaira, these are all lies, what you write". I had dreams about it too.'

She paused and shared, 'I would organise pages I had written on for posting the next day, and at night I would dream that they had caught fire. One day, I dreamt that I'd gone to the graveyard and all the papers I'd written my stories on were scattered there. These dreams didn't let me write.'

Dreams have an added significance for Sumaira because she often experiences events in her dream world that actually transpire in real life. For instance, she shared that often when she dreams of a relative's illness or passing away, she soon hears that the event has actually occurred. 'These make me scared.' Even little, everyday things such as dreaming of a certain dish being cooked for lunch:

the next day, the family without consciously doing so somehow end up making that dish.

'In the last dream I saw that the Prophet (PBUH) is standing by my pillow and holds out his hand. I place my hand in his, and then I thought [with enthusiasm], the hand that has been in his, how can I write lies [*jhoot*] with that hand?'

'But what if you write true stories, even then?'

'No, but even in true stories, you write so much from yourself. So my conscience was not satisfied.'

The anthropologist Amira Mittermaier (2010), in her ethnography on Cairo, aptly highlights the overlapping of the imagined and the 'real' when tracing the significance of dreams and their ethical, political, and religious implications. This is relevant for our purpose here because Sumaira's dream was about the Prophet Muhammad (PBUH) holding her hand. There was no clear signal to stop writing fiction, yet that dream led to a decision that has impacted her real life in terms of leading her to disengage from fiction.

Although Sumaira has stopped writing fiction, her creativity seems to be present and blooming in dreams. As she narrated her dreams to me, I could almost visualise the scenes: gatherings that depicted the Day of Judgment, visiting the third sky, patches of land that walked, baggage as large as a house.[4]

A sense of purity was a prominent motif in most of her dreams. For instance, in one she is warned of observing seventy veils, so when she lifts her veil, her face, along with those of her family's other women, is shining and free of scars. This is because they have taken care to protect their faces from men's gaze. The second significant motif was the power that is bestowed when a person makes the effort of frequently connecting with the divine. For instance, she shared that she recited *durood-e-taj* (verses in praise of the prophets) every day.

'Baji [Kulsoom] and all would stop me from it and tell me that the one who recites it for three years becomes a *sahib-e-kashf* [someone aware of the hidden]. But we are weak; we cannot bear the weight of the hidden [so I should not recite it]. I used to recite it up to a hundred times a day; I read it for eighteen months in the morning.'

Thus, the effort she had put into connecting with the divine had enriched her inner world, and her dreams had become richer and more fulfilling.

I had rarely seen her at the spontaneous social meetings that took place, so I asked her how she spent her day.

'Sometimes I do some housework, like cooking, but I recite *durood-e-paak* [a different verse in praise of prophets] a lot. Most of the day is spent talking.' She laughed, 'Isn't this a good life? Whatever I read about *aalim* or whatever I hear, I tell it to others.'

As she began to talk about her favourite religious scholars (ulema) her face lit up. She began to point out that spreading God's word (*tableegh*) was the best work in the world because distancing ourselves from religion (*be-deeni*) had made our hearts barren. Just as barren land has to be watered over and over again, sermons have to be listened to repeatedly. Her response to leaving fiction also had an analogy, of her heart not being in these things any longer (*dil nahi lagta ab aisay kaamon main*).[5]

As we spoke about her change in attitude toward fiction, her critique of digest writing was apparent, yet so was Simran's defence of it.

K: How do you feel about Kulsoom and Simran's writing now?

Sumaira: That's their problem/issue [*maslaa*]. When Allah gives enlightenment [*roshni*], it is up to him.

Simran, who had so far been silent, quickly added, 'Allah gives enlightenment in different ways'.

K: When did you experience this change?

Sumaira: About three years—before that, my inclination was that I would write a play, but then it changed. It's up to Allah whatever works he wants from us and whatever he wants us to leave.

'And whatever way he wants us to go, guidance [*hidayat*] can be in different ways,' added Simran.

There was also the sense of other people not really understanding what needed to be prioritised when she asked me about my routine in the US. As I began telling her about my day, instead of asking for more details or how I felt about living there (as most other writers did), she asked about what I thought of the Muslims there and then added that she felt they did not understand religion. As Simran and I spoke about how certain cultural values were seen as religious, Sumaira disagreed:

> No, but sometimes you also get coloured in the same colour. I've also heard of several cases. Like [the Urdu writer] Ata ul Haq Qasmi has written that he went to America and saw a girl in the mosque offering her prayers. She was wearing a short dress, and her legs were uncovered, but Islam tells you to cover yourself completely.

This sense of wanting to correct the behaviours she had seen or heard about had strong connotations of protectiveness. For instance, later in the year when she went for Umrah, she brought back a veil as a gift for me. Sumaira explained to her cousins that I was basically good, but she feared that lack of guidance about religion could lead to Allah's displeasure (and disappointments in my life). Her cousins persuaded her to send me a gift other than a veil as I would not use it. Nonetheless, her attempts to guide me in terms of eternal life continued in different ways. In this sense, then, her focus appears to be on what a person can gain for the afterlife, as this life is temporary and illusory.

During our visit to the mosque, most of the girls rapidly completed their prayers and trailed out to the courtyard. I leaned against the wall and waited for Simran and Sumaira, who stood praying in front of me. They were both performing the same set of prescribed motions (hands raised, forehead down, finger raised) yet each was doing it in her own way. Simran's motions were expansive, her body language lively, almost exuberant. In contrast, Sumaira's gestures and motions were gentle, silent, and inward. As I gazed at them, it appeared as if I was witnessing two lives with the same set of prescribed rules, yet each had appropriated those rules in her own way and created her own path for agency.

In the context of digest writing, for Simran, 'A story is conflict; it is a disagreement with the world you are given [*kahani ikhtilaf hoti hai*]. I tell people, "Change the world, and we won't have to write stories anymore".' Sumaira too is in disagreement but her approach has been to withdraw inward into her dream world. Thus, although both live their lives within prescribed norms, comparable to the set of prescribed prayer motions, the way each has chosen to give meaning to her existence has been different. For Sumaira, religion has become the path toward giving meaning to her existence, hence her rich dreams, withdrawal into an inner world and a focus on investing in eternal life. In contrast, Simran has sought to create meaning by reaching outward, open to experiencing and sharing whatever she experiences.

At one level, it is easy to funnel engagement with digests (or creative writing) as empowerment and agency, and disengagement as giving up on the possibility of change. However, as Mahmood (2001) aptly observes, agency understood as the capacity to realise our own interests against the weight of obstacles is only one point of view; there can be other historically or culturally specific notions of agency. In other words, the underlying assumptions we have about self-actualisation, empowerment, and agency come from a particular point of view and form our filters as we judge other women's choices in life. Thus, we need to take into account the 'desires, motivations, commitments, and aspirations' of the people to whom these choices are important (Mahmood, 2001: 225).

Digest writing for Madare Shah and Kulsoom became an avenue to access other women and sharing their 'vast or tiny longingful projections' (Humphrey, 2005: 43). These personal ruminations about djinns, *kari* women, and abandoned babies were social in that they were directed towards interpreting readers (our own consciousness or that of others) but also individual because they were written through particular personal filters and perceptions of reality. Sumaira attempted this path but then abandoned it and withdrew into her inner world. However, as her dreams indicate, this inner world is as engaging as (if not more than) the creative fiction she wrote earlier. In this sense, empowerment comes through writing for Kulsoom and Simran, but for Sumaira, it entails investment in her eternal life.

In this context, rather than a quick funnelling of these women's choices into 'good/bad', 'passive/active', there is a need to treat their choices with as much respect and authenticity as we would expect for our own priorities. Madare Shah, Kulsoom, and Simran have made choices which I celebrate as empowerment and self-actualisation. Yet from Sumaira's point of view, she is also empowered. Through her practices of connecting with the divine, she has created a position for herself where she can protect people like me, whom she sees as disempowered through a lack of religious knowledge.

As I write these last paragraphs, my recent conversation with Sumaira comes to mind. I had called her to ask if she wanted me to add anything to the section about her. 'No, I can't think of anything now,' she said offhandedly, and then added, '*Ami* is sending you her regards (salam).'

'Tell her I wear the dupatta she gave me almost all the time with shalwars and jeans.'

Sumaira seemed concerned and asked, 'Do you wear jeans?' She seemed relieved when I shared that I wore them with long shirts. 'Then it's okay, because otherwise [religiously], it is like putting your physical self on exhibition.' In a sense, she had given her message of *tableegh* and adhering to religious edicts. In this little example, her association took the form of empowering me through what she sees as the authentic form of agency: religious knowledge and getting me to invest in my eternal life.

Finally, this chapter demonstrates how different writers depict and engage with the same lived realities. I have highlighted the world of these writers and traced how each of them engages with this given world through her own lens and notions of agency and engagement. Madare Shah, Kulsoom, and Simran are creating meaning and giving coherence to their experiences by writing stories. For Sumaira, fiction is 'the world of lies', and silence and dreams are a meaning-making experience.

NOTES

1. These family members often shared an anecdote about him walking through the village with a small piece of cloth tied around his stick. Even little children would gather around him, asking him for pocket money. Because he did not want to hurt the children's feelings by saying 'no' to them, he would open the cloth and tie it around his stick to indicate that he had no money that day.

2. In this particular context, adoption has different connotations than that which we usually understand it to be. When a cousin or aunt adopts an infant, she raises the baby and has a significant voice in parental decisions about future marriage and education. However, because the family shares the same household, the child interacts daily with other siblings, and formal legal guardianship remains with the biological parents.

3. Pakhtuns are an ethnic group who come from the northern region of Pakistan.

4. Babri Mosque (built in the sixteenth century) was located in Uttar Pradesh, India. On 6 December 1992, it was demolished by right-wing Hindus who believed it to have been built over the birthplace of Lord Ram. This was followed by several months of intercommunal rioting between Hindu and Muslim communities in India, resulting in at least 2,000 fatalities.

5. One of the compulsory rituals during Hajj, called *saee*, involves walking between the two hills of Safa and Marwa to commemorate Bibi Hajra (the Prophet Abraham's [AS] wife), who made seven trips between these hills as she desperately searched for water for her son.

6. However, as a sign of respect, they are not directly referred to by that name but by the name used to refer to that elder. For instance, a fifteen-year-old who was named after her grandmother was called Wadi amma (respected mother). During my initial stay, this often led to amusing situations. I would

stand up each time I heard 'Wadi amma' being called to the room, only to find a young girl with a slightly surprised look at my efforts to pay respect.

7. Most of the younger cousins are now ardent digest readers. Of course, given the gap of three decades, what these young girls read and what Madare Shah read in this genre are very different. One obvious example is the shift from the oral to the visual, along with stories that weave in modern technology such as mobile phones and computers. In contrast, a typical story for Madare Shah and Apiya entailed a strong sense of the oral-tradition style of narration.

However, the most obvious difference is in terms of the way they engage with other readers. Madare Shah and Apiya did not have access to other writers or readers aside from the letters they sent to the digest office. The third generation, however, has direct access to other readers as well as writers through their smartphones.

'Kiran *api*, you should see the fights that happen on the writers' Facebook pages. Like this one novel had two heroines: Half the readers liked the older, mature one, but the other half liked the younger one, and both were not even willing to hear the name of the other one.'

'Some of the girls were Indians,' Laiba began to add to Fauzia's account. 'We know because we visited their profile page.' Moreover, every home now also has a satellite dish and television. These girls can therefore also watch television plays written by digest writers. Surprisingly, however, in most cases they choose not to watch these plays. This is because the visual portrayal usually contradicts how they imagined the characters. They seem to share these views with other readers, with whom they regularly interact through social media. Thus, although the girls' lives have the same parameters of physical access as Madare Shah's generation, they have other avenues of access to which Madare Shah's generation never did.

8. Her central argument is that there are two discourses used by Bedouins, one expressing honour and modesty and a contradictory one in which people express emotions that might usurp a position of honour. The apparent contradiction provides evidence for Abu Lughod's argument that 'it is impossible to reduce Bedouin "culture" to the official social and moral ideals encapsulated in the code of honour and modesty' (Abu Lughod, 1999: xvii).

The second section of discourse on sentiment, however, shows that Bedouins can and do buckle in their daily struggle to uphold those ideals; poetry is an important discourse that allows them the space to express some resistance against those ideals and their realities.

9. The women of the family are not allowed to attend regular school. However, Simran's maternal family does not practise this custom, so she has several

cousins who are formally educated. Through them and her brothers, she acquired textbooks for the primary level and then the ninth and tenth grade and used these to tutor her younger cousins and sisters. A few days after my return to Islamabad, her younger sister Fauzia, as well as two other cousins, had begun taking their matriculation exams privately. Her brothers were not in favour of this, viewing it as a breach of purdah, but Simran's father supported her in this initiative, so their objections were brushed aside. Fauzia's excitement was apparent when I called her to ask how the exam had gone: 'Kiran *api*, there were so many girls there, and the paper was tough, but we were together; Mahnoor and I stayed up last night so we could finish studying together.'

Whereas Fauzia's focus was on the experience of the exam itself, for Simran, this meant a huge step in terms of changing their familial norms and opening up opportunities for her sisters and cousins.

10. Her depiction of the Sindhi literary magazine office was surprisingly accurate even though she has never been in such a space. When I asked her how she depicted spaces she had never seen, she simply replied, 'There's the TV; there are people who talk about their rooms or spaces, so one gets an idea from that.'

11. Cognitively, we frame the mind and body as separate, yet empirical evidence consistently demonstrates the instability of this binary. Grosz gives the example of people who experience multiple personality disorder—each personality has its own bodily strengths and weaknesses (one person needs spectacles while another does not, even though it is the same set of eyes)—or the development of stigmata or perforations in people with strong religious beliefs. Another example that comes to mind is that of body dysmorphia: cases where individuals feel a specific limb has to be amputated to make their bodies habitable. These cases pose a conundrum for psychiatrists, as cognitive or psychoanalytical therapy does not really work here, which makes us wonder whether it is again the dynamism of the body taking over in some sense.

She articulates her model as a three-dimensional inverted figure 8 (which Lacan uses in a different context). For Grosz, the relationship is neither one of two substances nor two kinds of attributes of a single substance, but somewhere in between. Just as this figure has no clear boundaries, but the inner twists into and shapes the outer. One that resists as much as possible both dualism and monism. A model which insists on two surfaces which cannot be collapsed into one and which do not always harmoniously blend with and support each other. One, where the join, the interaction of the two surfaces, is always a question of power; a model which *may* [original emphasis] be represented by the geometrical form of the Mobius strip's two-dimensional torsion in three dimensional space. (Grosz, 1994: 189).

12. Djebar reworks traditional history in the novel by de-centring the dominant version of history of the Algerian struggle and brings to light women's voices and participation in the movement against French colonialism techniques.

13. A large percussion instrument.

14. *'Jab khuwab beh gaye'* (when dreams were swept away), *Sachi Kahaniyan* Digest, July 2011.

15. Dream 1: 'I heard Baji call out to me, and she is saying, "Sumaira, be careful. You have to be within seventy veils' *(sattar pardon main)*". I turn back and ask, "Where is the key to *Riaz ul jannah* [an area in the mosque built in the initial years of Islam]?" And I find out it's with (Pakistan's current prime minister) Nawaz Sharif, who is in Madina [laughing]. It's just a dream, and I take the key from him, and I move to *Mazar-e-Mubarik* (the grave of the Holy Prophet (PBUH)]. I lay my head down there and start to cry and recite *meetha meetha hai meray* Muhammad (PBUH) *ka naam* [a famous poem in praise of the Prophet] and then I woke up.'

Dream 2: 'We are all *bibiyan* [ladies] of this village, and there is an open ground, and we are all standing there. And my maternal uncle, who is a *maulana* [religious scholar], says, "You used to recite *durood-e-taaj* frequently, so now you have to cultivate this patch of land." I say, "How can I?" but then I recite *darood-e-taaj*, and the land becomes cultivated, and I ask the other women to recite Surah Yaseen. I recite it loudly, and the narrow street I am worried about passes through it, and then it starts to pass through water. And my maternal uncle says, "You should not do this," like it was with Moses. Everyone is scared, there is dust, and our little children are there. We have our bags, too, the size of houses. I'm scared in the dream because I feel like it's the picture of the Day of Judgment. As it walks, that patch of the land reaches heaven [Jannah], and the floor is of glass, and the sides are of gold and silver, and there I calmly come down and feel I've reached my destination.'

Dream 3: 'I saw that all the women have snacks *[samosay, mithai]* et cetera, in gold plates, and it's being distributed. There are huge mirrors, and I say, "Baji, let's see if our faces have a mark. We have a niqab," [veil] and Madare Shah says, "No, our faces are without any scars". Then I lift my niqab, and my face is clear.'

16. Sumaira usually watches the Quranic channel on TV but sometimes also watches plays. In plays, too, her taste is similar to her taste for *aalims*; she likes those that make an impression or have a message. Thus, the only one she watches regularly is a Turkish drama entitled *Masoom*. She shared that it's about 'the same problem we have in Pakistan about *watta satta*. This

little girl is married off, and then she has all these responsibilities of running the household and all. They even beat her, so it's because of this *mazloom* girl that I watch it.' Her interest in the play was also understandable because she preferred living a single life to one of a *watta satta* marriage.

4

In Quest of Respect: Engagement with the Electronic Media

There are certain terms that have a peculiar property. Ostensibly, they mark off specific concepts that lay claim to a vigorously objective validity. In practice, they label vague terrains of thought that shift or narrow or widen with the point of view of those whosoever makes use of them, embracing within their gamut of significances conceptions that not only do not harmonise but are in part contradictory.

— Edward Sapir (1951: 308).

The previous chapter demonstrates how women who lack access to mobility and institutionalised forms of education engage with digest fiction as an avenue for authentic self-expression. This chapter continues the story of digest writers by examining how they make sense of their entry into television and the challenges they have to face, in particular in relation to the social perception of not being 'real' writers. The first section begins by focusing on a popular drama serial to demonstrate the parallel dynamics, on the one hand, of commercial success and popularity, and on the other, of invalidity as writers. It explores the social perception of digest writers as pandering to the lowest common denominator. I suggest that although these plays do pander to certain commercial or base desires, the television depictions of digest fiction also act as an avenue for what can best be described as little slivers of reality:

personal experiences of middle-class women which they rescue from oblivion.

In this context, I present two plays: one of a digest writer, partly based on my personal life, and another which depicts the struggles of a digest writer who becomes a television script writer. I briefly compare the latter to a digest story written in the 1970s to highlight some similarities and differences in how digest writers have continued to address the notion of inauthenticity through their work. I present key themes to demonstrate that the struggle for authenticity is not just in the public realm but also the private one of family. Finally, I follow up on these two key strands, familial disapproval and challenges in the television arena, by narrowing the ethnographic gaze to two writers to show the specific forms these issues take in their lives.

CONTEXTUALISING AUTHENTICITY IN NEW ARENAS

Let me begin by sharing an exchange with a well-meaning family friend.

'So you're working on fiction writers: have you interviewed Nurul Huda Shah [a well-known, highbrow literary writer]?'

'No, my focus is on digest writers.'

'I know, it is often difficult to get these well-known literary people to give time.'

Halfway through fieldwork, I was by now used to the questions that often followed my focus on digest writers. People assumed that my work was a kind of critique on how their narratives pandered to the demand for easy reading or that I had to change my focus from literary, well-known writers to these women simply because it was methodologically easier to access them for interviews. I usually lost people's attention when I sought to justify my choice. I was therefore quite happy to have the opportunity to explain my point of view when a writer asked to interview me and share my research through her Urdu column. This writer, whom we will call Syema, used to write for digests but is currently active at literary fora. She confided that her identity as a digest writer usually causes problems of not having literary merit, so she often has to keep that aspect under wraps.

We had a long conversation about why I felt digest writers needed to be heard, and how class and gender dynamics play into the discourse of their inauthenticity. Syema shared that when she posted her published column on Facebook, it led to an aggressive debate because most members of the literary community felt that digest writers could not even be positioned as writers.

Digest writers position authenticity as a quality of experience; the ability to move another to tears or laughter, a certain sincerity of depiction; therefore, they see their writing as authentic. However, others, such as the English-language press or Urdu literary circles, continue to call them digest writers rather than writers or fiction writers. The subtext is that these writers are somehow not accomplished or 'real' writers because they write for digests. Usually, once a cultural good has been declared authentic, the demand for it rises, and it acquires a market value (Bendix, 1997: 7). In the context of digest writers, however, this does not hold true. In recent years, their narratives have achieved wider circulation through their work as scriptwriters for private television channels. The market value for their narratives has thus expanded to the visual sphere. This wider circulation has however also led to a wider discourse on their inauthenticity as writers. This is similar to what Sapir (1951: 308) eloquently calls 'vague terrains of thought that narrow or widen with the point of view of those whosoever makes use of them' regarding their work as writers. Their dramas portray their dreams and desires—and these are desires that appear to resonate with a large population, yet their perception as 'digest writers' rather than 'real writers' has grown more rigid.

Digest Writers in the Visual Arena of Television

Digest writers began working for television post 2002. In Pakistan, television began in 1964 and till 1996, there were only three channels. However, since 2002, factors such as licensing for private television channels have led to a proliferation of entertainment channels. Hum TV, ARY Digital, Express TV, GEO, and A Plus are some of the leading ones, and the bulk of airtime is given to televised serials. For instance, in any given week, the website *Dramas Online* broadcasts new uploaded episodes from 50–55 ongoing drama serials. Thus, whereas earlier a few selected writers associated with highbrow literary forms wrote most televised serials, now the proliferation of channels and their need to fill airtime has led to a variety of voices as well as genres in televised serials which were not prevalent earlier. One of the most popular among them is the televised form of digest narratives. Thus, digest writers have begun entering the field with a polyphonic voice on gender, family, and femininity.

Let me begin with a brief ethnographic note about meeting the head of Hum TV, the channel most digest writers aspire to work for:

As I walk into Hum TV's main office in Karachi, it appears spacious and modern with its white floor and black furniture. A little while later, I'm led to the executive director's office by the head herself, a woman with warm eyes and a welcoming demeanour. She addresses me as *bachay* (child) and shares that she initially worked as a host for children's shows and subsequently as a director for television dramas. The launch of her private channel had been fraught with problems. Other private channels were owned by established businesses and headed by men. Hers was the first one owned and headed by a woman. However, being a woman became a strength in the context of hiring digest writers. Familial concerns about script writing were quelled because the writers were interacting with a well-known, middle-aged woman rather than an unfamiliar man.

The channel head, Sultana Siddiqui, explains that the language used and themes adopted by digest writers were relatable and familiar to people at large, so they began employing them for script writing.

> People sometimes tell me that the plays are retrogressive, but we always show strong women characters. Also, I always make it a point to ensure that serious issues should not become spectacles. For instance, if you are portraying rape, you should not make it into a spectacle but focus on the pain that the girl and her family undergo.

I silently wonder how a script based on Siddiqui's own life would be received. In a sense, her life sharply contrasts with the plays her channel is often critiqued for airing. As the first to employ digest writers, Siddiqui broke the hold that highbrow literary writers had on television screens. Yet simultaneously, her channel has attracted criticism for airing dramas that are viewed as pandering to people's desires for frivolous entertainment. As we speak, her office wall displays several television screens, each beaming a different channel. I glance at a screen beaming a rerun of the popular television serial *Humsafar*, a serial which played a key role in circulating digest writers' notions of womanhood and the subsequent criticism of them undermining women's agency.

Humsafar is a television drama serial based on a novel written by a digest writer who later turned it into a television script. As I elaborate in the following paragraphs, it proved to be immensely popular but also led to critiques of digest writers and their work.

HUMSAFAR: POPULARLY ACCEPTED BUT NOT RESPECTED

Aired from September 2011 to March 2012, this 15-episode drama serial revolves around an estranged couple. An engineer by

training, 30 year-old digest writer Farhat Ishtiaq originally wrote
it as a novel.[1] 'I was sitting on the sofa with my sister watching
TV, and this song came on: "He was a companion, but we lacked
familiarity/there were shadows and there was light, there was
no separation".'[2] These lyrics were originally written by Naseer
Turabi in 1971, after Bangladesh separated from Pakistan. For
Ishtiaq, however, it evoked the idea of misunderstandings between
married couples. This led to the two main characters: a socially
well-established man named Ashar and his wife, Khirad, who is
from a middle-class family. Rather than romance that leads up
to marriage, the drama explores the theme of falling in love after
marriage.[3]

Ishtiaq tells me that two production houses rejected her script
on the basis that audiences would not relate well to a husband-and-
wife romance story. However, Hum TV's Momina Duraid (Sultana
Siddiqui's daughter-in-law) decided to take this risk. As Farhat
shares her story, it evokes some strands of Khirad's trajectory:
entering unfamiliar, socially privileged groups, being seen as
socially and intellectually inauthentic, and then, finally, acceptance.
Khirad's happy reunion with Ashar is mirrored in Farhat's union
with Hum TV and the popularity of the drama serial that exceeded
expectations. Nationally, it received one of the highest rated TRPs
(a tracking system for calculating the percentage of television
audience for a specific show). This was the highest in recent years
and led to the Hum TV Phenomenal Serial Award. The audience
crosses age boundaries: a popular YouTube video shows two six-
year-olds arguing with each other about whether Ashar is a good
person.[4] On social media, a Facebook group was created called 'If
a Girl Ditches an Episode of Humsafar to Talk to You, Then Marry
Her'. The official Facebook page for the show itself had over 141,000
likes, and the quotes and photos posted on the wall had individually
garnered thousands of likes. Similarly, there is a separate Facebook
page called 'Ashar and Khirad' which presents interaction between
the key characters as Facebook friends. Internationally, the play

was aired and rerun on Indian television channels and also became the first Pakistani serial to be aired on Middle Eastern television.

As the play circulated, along with its commercial success and popularity, there arose a parallel reaction of ridicule. YouTube parodies of the play proliferated, and in particular the English-language press, highlighted it as undermining women's agency. It was contrasted with plays from the 1980s penned by highbrow, literary writers, and a subsequent discourse of how audience tastes had changed for the worse began proliferating in television magazines. As digest writers' ideas of womanhood and desires dominated the screen, it was seen as derailing Pakistani women's hard-earned independence. Some also pointed out how the middle-class female protagonist was set against and portrayed as being better than the upper-class, English-speaking woman, the implication being that middle-class notions of ideal femininity had spilled over from digest discourse on to television screens and were corroding liberal notions of womanhood. The tone of this discourse was in sync with the long-running, earlier concern about digest narratives and the negative impact on readers' notions of women's independence and agency. The subtext here was that digest writers were not really authentic writers, and their desires, portrayed through their scripts, had a detrimental impact.

Arvind Rajagopal (2001) aptly observes that media neither cause nor reflect reality but participate in it and in the process reshape the context in which issues are conceived and understood. This observation becomes relevant for our purpose, as the popularity of this play led to both a wider audience and a subsequent wider critique of desires and dreams portrayed in digest narratives. Yet the space created by the success of these television plays has also allowed a particular vantage point, a kind of ethnographic gaze, a privileging of experiences that might not have otherwise made it to the screen.

OVERTURNING THE ETHNOGRAPHIC GAZE

Let me begin by sharing the experience of having the ethnographic gaze turn toward me and becoming the examined rather than the examiner.

'I thought your plot line and some of the depicted incidents sounded similar to a family I know; the similarities were striking,' I told a digest and script writer during a late-night conversation.

'You're right; it is based on a real marriage.'

Later, she quietly asked me why my marriage had ended. My answer led to further questions:

'What was it like when he came to see you?' 'How did your family react?' Over the next few hours, I found myself sharing some things I had not even disclosed to close friends.

After that summer of fieldwork, I went back to the usual rhythm of university life. One afternoon, I settled in to watch her new play. The opening scene showed a woman who sat in the courtyard, engaged in breathing exercises.

'Kiran, why can't you do this someplace else?' Naming a primary character after a friend is a gesture of affection, so it was flattering to see the writer had chosen my name.

As the play progressed, I gradually began to recognise some echoes of my conversations with the writer. Kiran on the screen was a product of the writer's imagination. Her circumstances, familial circle, and age were different from my life. However, the emotional conundrums she faced echoed those I had shared with her. Thus, her inner world, in particular the texture of her relationships and her emotional reactions, were very similar to those I had shared with the writer about myself. In other words, although that Kiran did not exist in real life, the emotional world depicted through her did.

This is not a unique occurrence. Digest writers occasionally base their stories on people they have encountered. To protect privacy, identifiable details are changed but the shared feelings are portrayed. Thus, the person who has shared her sentiments is aware that she has been woven into a portrayal, but her real identity remains confidential. What was perhaps unique here is the overturning of my assumption that the ethnographic gaze was one-way. My gaze was not just reciprocated but led to a representation. Our interaction had led to not one but two creations: ethnographic writing and a television script. At one level, they are markedly different in terms of content, circulation, and form. One path is of observation and the other of imagination. As a fiction writer, she was entitled to sculpt real life as she chose. In contrast, as an ethnographer I was restricted to the bounds of reality and was expected to take into account all aspects of what I observed.

My notes claimed to portray 'what is', whereas her play was presented as fictional 'what could be'. This binary is not, however, airtight. Her play was fictional but, as stated earlier, several emotional responses and dialogues were drawn from what actually happened. Similarly, this ethnography aims to present 'what is', but it is through a filter of subjective interpretation. What the respondents communicated forms the content of this work but some narratives were selected and others never made it past the transcription file. There is also the factor of underplaying certain aspects while accentuating others. Therefore, although the depiction is presented as fictional in one case and real in another, ultimately, each is a portrayal and thus assembled and created in a certain sense. What each desires of the audience is also similar. This writing aims at translation and carries an invitation to 'notice this, look at that' in an attempt to communicate the richness of the world of digest writers. Like all other ethnographies, this one implicitly asks its audience to step into a different world and wishes them to feel its flow and depth.[5]

The play too asks its audience to step into a different world, but in this case, it is one of feelings. This work is about observing and demonstrating, and that is about imagining and feeling, but the underlying invitation placed before the audience to share that gaze is common. Let us turn to the anthropologist Didier Fassin here, as his reflections on true lives and real lives help us understand some other hidden parallels.[6] He delineates between truth and reality as 'concepts in profound and permanent tension' rather than interchangeable or equivalent notions (Fassin, 2014: 42). The real is essentially what has happened or exists in actual life, whereas the true is that which has to be retrieved and reclaimed from convention. Thus, reality is horizontal because it exists on 'the surface of facts', and truth is vertical because it can only be discovered 'in the depths of inquiry'. He suggests that anthropologists present what happened in a particular community or individual life, whereas artists strive to grasp the life that may escape even the person who lives it and 'rescue it not so much from death or oblivion as from insignificance' (2014: 53).[7] In this context, the play lent authenticity to certain moments of my own life which I had relegated as insignificant.

What about the depictions digest writers have about their own experiences in the wider arena of television, and what are the moments that are brought forth 'rescued from insignificance'? In the next section, I explore this question by selecting some key themes from a play written by a digest writer about the challenges of becoming a script writer. It is not surprising that one of the key themes is addressing and responding to notions of inauthenticity. Thus, although digest writers lack a voice in literary fora as well as the English-language press, they do speak to notions of inauthenticity but through the medium they know best: fiction.

'HANDS THAT CHOP GARLIC CAN NEVER WRITE A WORTHWHILE SENTENCE'? DIGEST WRITERS RESPOND

The drama serial entitled *Digest Writer* aired from October 2014 to March 2015 and was written by a relatively junior digest writer by the name of Madiha Shahid.[8] Both the production house, Larachi Entertainment, and the channel that aired it, Hum TV, have produced several plays written by digest writers. This, however, was the first time that a play focused on the life of a digest writer.[9]

> How can hands that chop vegetables and cook write a worthy sentence or a worthy story? This can be a coincidence or good luck, but not talent. Because talent is that which is written in solitude late at night on an expensive study desk. The women who change dirty diapers and peel garlic and ginger can't create. The ordinary public sees itself in our plays, but our literary writers [adeeb] and journalists find our characters irritating. Our heroes and heroines are not realistic, but is there anyone who has never gone into an inner or imaginary world? Stop the abuse and exploitation of women in your society, and the women in the plays written by digest writers will also change, and till that happens, watch and read our writing with the same respect that is afforded to other writers.

The central character, Fareeda, a digest writer, delivers these lines at a channel event. However, during her speech, the camera pans repeatedly to male content department head and highbrow writer Mazhar Hayat, who is portrayed as a writer known for his literary skills. As an intellectual, Hayat is depicted as resentful and disdainful of digest writers' popularity. However, he needs to increase ratings for his channel and has to contact digest writers. Therefore there are financial gains to be had in hiring digest writers, but this is done with a sense of disdain. In one scene, sitting in his leather office chair, Hayat asks his assistant if he has contacted any 'real writers' or whether they are all digest writers.

> MH: Did you call that writer Rashk-i Hina [Pride of Henna]? Such strange names these women use for themselves!
> A: Yes, she couldn't believe I was calling from your office. She is a huge fan of your work. She will send the one-liner in three days and then the serial in about a month.
> MH: [Sighing] We used to take years writing serials, and these women feel it is complete within a month.

Later, he calls her.

MH: What kind of a story is this? A woman and a man both from the elite class and their romance—where are the problems of real life, where are the struggles? You just have romance; the hero is running after the girl in a BMW, gifting her diamond rings, bringing her flowers.

As Fareeda gradually becomes a television script writer, her domestic work continues to interweave with her creative writing. While the money is used to meet household expenses, she is also expected to take responsibility for all the household chores. Her writing is, therefore, mostly done in the kitchen. In one particular scene, the camera pans across her handwritten page and her meditative expression. Her attention is suddenly diverted by something. The camera changes its angle, and instead of the expected writing table, we see a kitchen counter and a stove with frying onions.

In a subsequent scene, we see the well-furnished television channel's office, where Hayat holds her handwritten page in his hand and shakes his head.

This page, smelling of garlic and ginger, and decorated with oil stains. These women think that they can become writers. Writers write alone, at night. These women can't become writers by sitting in the kitchen ... I wish I wasn't alive to witness this day.

He calls Fareeda, and after his (now regular) lecture to her to work hard, tells her to send 'cleaner' work, as her pages stink of garlic and ginger and are stained with cooking oil.

The world of literary circles and channels is not the only arena where writers strive for respect and authenticity. As the play aptly demonstrates, the familial realm too is fraught with problems.[10]

In the very first scene, the camera pans across a room lit by a reading lamp and a woman's voice relates a story about a man and a woman who are walking together. 'Faria walked around the place admiring its beauty while Nofil stood gazing at the joy and excitement on her face.' In contrast, the room we see is dimly lit, functional, and occupied by two sleeping girls aside from Fareeda, who is writing the story.

The contrast between the story Fareeda relates to us and her own life becomes stark when her father wakes up and enters her room. Her narration and vivid expressions of unconditional love and romance are disrupted when we witness his cold anger. 'Why are you up so late? What work is this that can't be done during the day? The electricity bill is already so high.' She lies and tells him she is studying for a test she could not study for earlier because her evening was taken up by tutoring children and cooking dinner. He brushes this off and tells her that he does not want her to study beyond BA (Bachelors of Arts) because it creates problems in finding a good match. He adds that she should offer her morning prayers now as it is almost time for sunrise. The scene ends when we hear her quiet 'Okay'.

The other key colour in this tapestry is the secrecy and struggle that surrounds her efforts to have her stories published in a digest.[11] A few days later, her story is published, and the ripple effect it has on her life is portrayed through various key scenes. Initially, we witness her excitement when she reads her published story over and over again and shares the news with her mother and sisters.

> Shakeela (Fareeda's sister): Ammi, her story has been published.
> Ammi: What? What story? What is it about?
> Jameela (Fareeda's sister): Ammi, I'll tell you; it's about a girl and boy and their romance. They have an affair [*unn ka chakkar chal jaata hai*]. All kinds of things about passion and romance are in it.
> Ammi: (Angrily) Don't you feel ashamed writing such stuff? How dare you? If your father finds out, there will be hell to pay. He's not that spineless. I can't find good proposals for you, anyway; now, when people read these stories, they'll say, 'It's the parents' fault. They haven't raised her properly.'

Fareeda: It's not just about love and romance; there are also other things in it. There is entertainment for people and also moral lessons.

Ammi: Stop it; don't try to lecture me. People will wonder what kind of ideas are in this girl's head.

Shakeela: But it's a skill, and not everyone has it; writing too is a skill.

Ammi: Just stop it. A skill for a girl is in the household tasks she can perform.

Muttering to herself, the mother leaves the room while a subdued Fareeda crosses over and sits alone.

Why are these scenes important, and what do they reflect? Each work explores existence from a particular vantage point and invites its audience to experience life from that perspective. In this context, the very fact that the play was written, produced, and widely watched proclaims unspoken that 'this too matters', 'this' being the lives of digest readers and writers and their perspectives. The familial disapproval of digest-related work, the burden of kitchen work, exploitation by production houses and such micro-experiences and realities are all rescued from oblivion and raised to a level of some significance as digest writers' thoughts and dreams circulate. Perhaps, in the final analysis, the struggle for respect is not about writing at all but the significance of these micro-realities of their everyday existence as women.

It is interesting to compare notions of disrespect enunciated in the play *Digest Writer* to a short story written in 1985 which deals with the same theme of familial disapproval and not being viewed as 'real' writers. The story, 'A Thousand Scars of the Fragile Heart', revolves around a young digest writer named Bazgha.

Bazgha's younger sister, Bilqees, walked in, holding the digest Bazgha's story was published in.

'Bhaiya [brother], Baji's story has been published—but in a digest.'

Bazgha's joyous mood was spoiled. 'Where else should it have been published? *Heavenly Ornaments* [a religious book for the education of women]?'[12]

'Baji, if it had been published in a literary magazine, it would have been a big deal. People don't even consider digest writing to be literary [*adabi*]. Look at the people in your own home.'

'Okay.' She elongated her syllables and glanced at her younger sister in disbelief. 'What about the various digests around your bed? Then you should also read quality literature; why are you reading digests?' ...

'Bilqees begum, I'm not one to divide literature into boxes, and neither have I been successful in judging who can be designated a small writer and who a senior one. Time decides who has been sincere with their work and who has invested blood and tears [*khoon-i-jigar*] into their writing. The one who suffers from this pain [*jo iss dard main mubtala hota hai*] finds some way. The ones who write for digests write the same way as the guardians of literature [*adab ke thekedar*]. And also tell me, what do you actually mean by a literary magazine?'

Adeem asked, 'Have you read the big names in literature? What do you think about them?'

'My point is that you can write on whichever topic you want, but if you've written it well, then one stratum [*tabqa*] or another will definitely like it. This stratum might be big, or it might be small. What measuring tape do you have with which you can measure the minds of people? If your creations are good and well-liked, they will make a place for themselves, no matter what. And if they don't have the capacity to thrive and take root, they will end.'

Unlike Fareeda, who endures struggles with the outside world, Bazgha gains validation and a sense of worth.

Her creations were getting published. The phone would ring daily with calls only for her. A new magazine would only start once she guaranteed them she would contribute. But the place where she never heard a word of praise was at home. It seemed like every single member of her family was very angry with her [*sakht naraaz*], as if she had terribly mistreated each of them. Whenever the phone rang, all her sisters would say, 'You pick it up; it'll be for you.'

An additional problem was that her maternal aunt was married to her father's brother; all the relations were linked to the joint family, and it was a task to maintain them.

One evening, as she sat gazing at the stars, Adeem arrived. 'Have you heard? Uncle Asghar is extremely angry with you. He's coming over tomorrow morning to take you to task [*khaal khainnchnay*]. What stupid things do you write? This is why I keep telling you to read books.'

She deeply admired Uncle Asghar. Few people loved their own father as much as she loved Uncle Asghar. Respect, love, reverence [*aqeedat, izzat, mohabbat*]—she showered all these sentiments over him generously.

'You've written a short story about Uncle Asghar, and everything is true in it. He was angry that you have disrespected him in front of the world.' He laughed sarcastically.

'Oh, my God [*haaye main marr jaoon*]. I have not written about him at all. And Adeem, just think, why would I write about him?' She was very nervous now; it felt as if there was no blood running through her veins any longer [*kaato toh badan main lahoo nahi*], and her heart beat loudly.

Deeply hurt, she got up and picked up her short story and was surprised. How? But many things were similar to Uncle Asghar. And then, in a flash, she realised that all the qualities she had written were encompassed in him. She had written about her ideal, and the form it took was that of Uncle Asghar. Whatever was in her mind, she continued to write, write, and write, and even those things that should not have been written were on paper now. She got really angry with herself, but what was done was done. For several days she couldn't pluck up the courage to face Uncle Asghar. But he was a wise man. He understood that writers are mad; they just write, but the flow of the seas takes everything with them, and it's best to forgive them. But she felt deeply regretful, and this regret would perhaps be hers for the rest of her life.

There are problems with her readers too. She receives a letter from a man who blames her for the fights between his two wives. She begins to think of not writing any longer, but another letter from a woman makes her change her mind.

When you write, each wound seems like my own; every sorrow becomes new. What does your pen hold that you call forth my soul as you do? May God bless you, and keep writing—you will become eternal [*amr ho jao gi*].

Bazgha wept. 'I can't stop writing—dear God, why have you filled my heart with this pain? Why have you made this small lump so sensitive that it drowns me?'

It was a beautiful evening, and it had been organised to honour her. She didn't speak much about her fame at home. However, with her father's encouragement and approval, she often attended such occasions which were a source of honour not just for her but her entire family. On this beautiful occasion, she thought, 'I'll take Adeem along. That way, he'll get an idea of my stature and position. My identity is the sole result of my own efforts and my own work, and those disputing it will be seen as an enemy.'

She was showered with flowers. She sat quietly listening to her admirers. Each word was steeped in reverence. This delight [*kaif masti surroor*] permeated her being like blood flowing through veins. Suddenly, she heard her name on the mike. She was being invited to respond to questions by the audience. She had become so privileged [*mothabir*] with the love of these people. Nature or destiny [*qudrat*] had brought her here.

A voice from the audience asked her why digest fiction was not considered good literature. Bazgha remained silent for a few moments and then replied, 'I think literature is literature; it cannot be confined to the magazine in which it is published. Digests are read in every home, and what can be a greater service for literature? In today's busy world, for very few rupees, the varying colours of life are revealed. The literary magazines are caught up in a class system of sorts. High-brow literary creations are made available to people with high literary tastes once or twice a year, in such a limited quantity that they are distributed as holy manna [*tabarruk* ke taur par], and under the rule of 'first the privileged, and then the rest' [aval khuvaish baad darvaish]; we cannot access them. The writer of today is close to you; her problems and yours are similar. Her writings are lit up with the light of reality. Stories drawn from events taking place around us might not have sophisticated metaphors and language, but they do have earnest observation.'

'Oh Bibi, where are you going so dressed up? A young girl dressing up to go to meet unrelated people. God knows what's got into Usman [Abu]!' This was her aunt's consistent reaction [takia-i kalam].

She remained silent and, shaking her head, walked away. What do they know of the pull [nasha] of respect and fame? The outside world sang her praises but she yearned for a few kind words from members of her family. Any problem she faced was attributed to her work as a writer, even when her eyes hurt—that too was seen as being caused by digest writing.

The entire day her back hurt because of domestic responsibilities. But no one took that into account.

'She doesn't care about home or her siblings. Her life revolves only around herself and her room,' Ammi lamented.

Her heart filled with deep sadness. 'So should I stop writing? What should I do, dear God [ya Allah]? Never! I'll die if I stop writing.' With this thought, she bore everything.

Her Fridays involved giving the children in the family a bath, washing the floors, applying henna to her mother's and aunt's hair, making endless cups of tea, and cooking something nice, especially for her father. The last task was her own wish.

Everyone in the family gave her a hard time [ghaseettay thay] on the basis of this one weakness, as if she wasn't a fiction writer but a girl of loose morals. Her heart would pound for no reason. Holding her heart, full of holes from the snide remarks, she tried to remain busy and began to give the children a bath earlier than usual that day.

The radio was turned on. Some respected personality was being interviewed. The interviewer asked, 'Who do you think is writing well these days?'

Bazgha's heart grew still. She had put soap in Guddo's hair, but she stopped and listened intently.

'Among today's writers, Bazgha Hasan has the spark that can turn into a flame.'

What he said after this is not known as she ran and hugged Abu. 'Your prayers have given me this position. I'm so lucky.'

Abu patted her back. 'For sure.'

Suddenly she heard her mother. 'May you be blighted [*tera sathya naas*]! Can't you manage anything aside from fiction? Guddo is raising hell; you've filled his nose, eyes, and mouth with soap and are now busy basking in your fame.'

Her joy vanished. Ammi was really angry with her.

'Baji, did you hear? He was praising you so much. I went mad with joy.'

Shahida had always genuinely sided with her.

'What did you say?" Adeem joined them. 'I was also listening to the programme. No need to be so happy. He was talking about Basma Hasan.' He held out a collection of short stories. 'This writer. Don't know why you imagine such things [*khush fehmian*].'

'By the way, why were you listening so intently?' Bazgha asked him, emphasising every word slowly [*chuba chuba kar*].

'Shut up, Bazgha. It has nothing to do with you; I listen to it every Friday.'

'You listen to it because of me. You're jealous of me and scared of my fame. You can't admit it openly, but actually you are.'

Everyone was listening intently. Khala [aunt] gasped. 'He's going to be your husband!'

'Don't say a word. I will never marry him. He will spend the rest of his life in ideological toil.' Having said this, Bazgha ran crying to her room.

Her father sat with his head in his hands. An average, middle-class household's average girl's thinking had grown too lofty [*soch bauhat buland ho gayi thi*]. All the family members' eyes were on Abu, who sat thinking, 'This girl has taken undue advantage of the liberty given to her.'[13]

It is interesting to compare these two works in the context of the current larger circulation and subsequent discourse of digest writers' inauthenticity. Both works of fiction depict the theme of familial disapproval. There are however some key differences, particularly in how the 'outside' is positioned. In the short story, it is a source of validation. Bazgha feels secure and validated by the outside (represented by the digest office, editors, and literary writers). By contrast, for Fareeda the outside too is a place of struggle for authenticity. Bazgha's principal critic is within her family, her fiancé, whereas Fareeda has to struggle with both the inner familial circle as well as the outside, represented by a literary writer. In other words, for Bazgha the literary writer is a source of validation, but for Fareeda he is a jealous competitor. This mirrors the dynamics of digest writers' entry into television, as they now compete in a new arena that was previously the sole domain of literary writers.

In the previous section, I have narrated the story digest writers tell about their own lives. In the following section, I shift gears to highlight how the two key themes, familial disapproval and inauthenticity, take specific forms in individual lives by narrowing the ethnographic gaze to two writers.

We have already met the first writer, Simran, a member of the Sindhi family introduced in the last chapter. We explored her engagement with fiction as a means of experiencing different feelings or examining specific questions. One of the aspects we traced was that, through her characters (such as Amrit, who works as an editor), she is able to explore possibilities which are unavailable in her everyday life. Writing about the fictional character of Amrit becomes an avenue that enables her to vicariously experience the toil of paid employment, workload, and career. The recent opening of the television arena to digest writers has created an opportunity where Simran can now explore the opportunities paid employment frequently brings. This is not, however, without problems. In the following paragraphs, we will explore her work as a script writer and the issues she has had to face in consequence.

SIMRAN: BLURRING LINES BETWEEN HALAL AND HARAAM

Simran's move into television has entailed having simultaneously to cope with two new pressures: having to manoeuvre a new environment with its commercial dynamics and facing familial disapproval. In the first case, the perception of not being a 'real' writer stems from being a digest writer, with its own connotations of being middle-class and somewhat less polished in terms of lack of fluency in the English language or asserting herself. In the second instance, it stems from venturing out into a field that is seen as un-Islamic. In this context, the community of readers and writers has become the space where she feels validated. In the next few paragraphs, I outline some forms of support which have helped her explore the avenue of script writing.

Notwithstanding problems of mobility and lack of formal education, Simran has been able to carve a path toward financial independence through television script writing. As a digest writer, she was paid very little (about Rs 1,000 or $10 for a short story). Serial novels have a better compensation rate (Rs 20,000–30,000 or $300). However, once they are published in book form, the royalty usually goes to the digest owners rather than the writers. Thus, digest writing itself is not financially lucrative, so for many writers like Simran, the avenue for financial independence is through script writing.

According to Simran's familial values and background as belonging to a family of religious saints, television is viewed as being un-Islamic. Their household now possesses television sets, and I would frequently find family members huddled around the television screen watching a drama. However, until the previous generation, television was forbidden. As Simran's aunt related,

My father sobbed and had tears in his eyes when he unexpectedly walked in and saw us watching television in my cousin's house. He cried, 'Our Syed daughters are being exposed to unfamiliar men [*namehram*] through their gaze'.

Over the years, television has become more acceptable. However, income earned through television is still considered haram and invalid in Simran's family. Simran's father supported her in her efforts to become a script writer. His support protected her from objections of other family members. After his unexpected death, her efforts are tolerated but not favourably regarded. The older generation in particular sees Simran's work for television as pushing the boundaries of Islamic codes of halal (valid/approved) and haram (forbidden/invalid) and often reminds her that the money earned from working for television is invalid [Television *ki kamai* haram *ki hoti hai*]. Thus, although she has become an earning member of the household, the respect that accompanies that status is missing. This familial pressure has led Simran to win over her disgruntled family members by visible displays of respect and acceptance of their authority. As she shared one day,

> Apa has been aloof toward me. I've been busy with script writing despite her opinion that it is Islamic-ly invalid. But that day, when she was lying down, I went in and began massaging her feet. She tried to resist, but I held them, saying, "Aren't you my mother?" And then she softened.

Holding someone's feet is a demonstration of the utmost respect for that person and an unconditional acceptance of their authority. Thus, rather than adopting a confrontational approach by engaging verbally, negotiating, and presenting her point of view, Simran has been able to continue with script writing by openly demonstrating her unconditional respect for disapproving family members.

These qualities have helped her to successfully manoeuvre through her family but dealing with production houses and

channels requires a very different set of skills. In the familial
context, being humble and self-effacing has helped her. However,
the same qualities of humility and self-effacement have become
a hindrance in the context of her negotiations with channels and
production houses. Other digest writers who are already in the
field have rallied around her and offered support in various forms.

Simran entered the foray of electronic media through Raheela, a
well-known senior digest writer and (now) script writer (introduced
in 'Chapter 1'). She recognised Simran's talent and helped her
develop a plot line for a play, commonly termed a one-liner. Simran
submitted it to the content department at a channel's production
house. When she attempted to follow up, the person at the content
department told her there were currently no productions underway.
'No one is that ignorant' [koi bhi itna jaahil nahi hota],' she shared
with sadness and anger. Simran felt that the content department
viewed her as someone who was from a small village and could
easily be manipulated. One of her principal concerns was that the
one-liner might have been given to another writer for development
into a script (a common occurrence because writers are usually
unable to avail of copyright law protection). 'I told Raheela, it's a
production house; to survive financially it needs to have ongoing
productions, so the story of no work is not possible.' Raheela agreed
and offered to help. Simran asked her to check with the head of
the production house to see if the one-liner had been submitted
under her name. They could not trace it, so she got the number of
the other production house's head from another senior digest and
script writer, Shehnaz. This executive director was surprisingly
supportive; she tried to trace the one-liner and told Simran none
of the production houses had it or at least not under her name.

Contacting the head proved to be a lucky break because the
executive director shared Simran's desire to have a story based on
rural Sindhi culture rather than the urban stories which dominate
the screen. They have been having conversations about which one
of her digest stories can be developed into a play. Although this

has not materialised yet, Simran has been contracted for another script. Because of Raheela's reputation as a successful script writer, her association with any project entails instant approval by the channels. Thus, one of the ways she supports talented junior writers is by developing one-liners (summary of the plot and characters) and having them write the actual script. She supervises them during the process, but the play is aired under the junior writer's name, which in turn helps them to contract other scripts (and better compensation rates). In this context, she offered Simran work on a play where the characters are Sindhi. Half the play is based in a Sindhi village, and the other half takes place in the US. Given Simran's familiarity with Sindhi culture, she is working on the scenes for the first half, and the other scriptwriter is working on the scenes based in the US. This has enabled Simran to rectify several stereotypes that might have gone unnoticed.

> Raheela and Kashaf wanted to add a scene about the hero struggling with an electric kettle in the US, and I told them, 'He's a medical doctor, so even if he's from a village in Sindh, he would be used to electric kettles'. Also, there was another scene about a mother complaining about her daughter to the neighbours, and that's not right either, because in the village, a mother will always try to hide her daughter's faults. She would never talk about them publicly.

As I listened to Simran's corrections, I was reminded of my own misguided stereotypes and assumptions drawn from television plays in the 1980s about Sindhi rural culture. At that time most of the plays were written by a few, often Urdu-speaking, writers. Their depiction of Sindhi rural households had led me to expect a dark, dingy haveli and depressed women.[14] The reality of Simran's household was very different, and a part of me perhaps was aware that it would be but the childhood image of those scenes had remained with me as a kind of mental hook or a reference point which I ended up comparing with my actual experience. In this context, Simran's voice helps provide a somewhat 'authentic' representation as well as a response, filtering out stereotypes which might have otherwise made it to the screen. The larger point I am making here is that a few decades ago a few writers dominated the screen, and their depictions carried traces of their own class, gender, and ethnic biases. Digest writers come from a variety of ethnic backgrounds, and therefore their depictions often overturn the earlier prevalent dominant ethnic stereotypes.

The three writers have now been working together on the script for over a year but have never met in person; WhatsApp messages and phone calls carry the work forward. Each writer sends her part of the script through WhatsApp to the other. This entails writing the scenes as well as 'cut offs' (transitions from one scene to another). The next step entails sending them to Raheela, who approves the version or suggests changes. Although the process sounds clear, there are several complications. For instance, Simran's qualities of forbearance and covering another's errors often lead her to complete the work Kashaf is supposed to do or take the blame for her mistakes. Their meetings take place through conference calls, so, often when Raheela objects to a scene, rather than clarifying that it was Kashaf's idea, Simran quietly takes the blame. Similarly, she often ends up writing scenes which Kashaf is supposed to work on.

During one such incident of delayed work by Kashaf, Simran began her phone conversation with me by asking me about US airports. 'See, I'm writing the scenes where Sarang has just arrived in the US. What was the airport like when you landed there?'

'I could send you links to YouTube videos of the airport,' I replied, thinking it might help to provide a larger perspective.

'Yes, send that, but tell me, how did it appear to you?'

'Shiny, with a lot of movement; people were walking very quickly.'

'What were you feeling and thinking about?'

I began to share my anxiety about the immigration process and worried thoughts about whether I had all the required documents. These were moments from the past which I had experienced, but Simran's questions reclaimed the significance of how those moments appeared to me. In a sense, we both relived those moments together; the experience of being at a US airport was mine, but Simran's capacity for feeling made it hers to. However, whether it makes it to an actual scene of the main character's landing at the airport is contingent on the channel budget.

Given the larger visual circulation, Simran is able to add her voice to correct certain misperceptions about Sindhi rural culture. Yet the freedom that she had in digest writing to explore whichever characters she wished (live whatever lives she wanted), lead them to whatever spaces or situations she wanted, is no longer there. The characters and turning points in the story have to fall within the frames of budget constraints and what the channel suggests. To take a simple example, digest narratives often depict large families; characters have many siblings and cousins around them. In the television arena, supporting characters have to be kept to a minimum because of budget issues. Another example is, as a script writer aptly stated, 'So our characters walk from the drawing room to the bedroom to the kitchen all day; we can't even show them going outside [because then the production costs increase]'.

Aside from the challenges any new work entails, Simran has also had to struggle with problems other junior writers usually do not face. A key problem was signing the contract, because she didn't have a national identity card.[15] When her work was restricted to digest writing, she was part of an informal public, where payments are made through money orders sent to the writer's address. In contrast, in the electronic media, one has to sign a formal contract. Simran's father's Pakistani citizenship card had expired, and her own could only be made once his was renewed. This took time, and being perceived as someone who didn't have an ID card caused her concern.

Digest writers have a following of readers and are often highly respected and looked up to by them. Entry into television entails dealing with a separate set of groups who do not perceive them as 'real' writers. As one writer described it, 'We don't have the glamour that people working for television have' (*hum main voh chamak nahi hoti hai*). Simran, like most digest writers, sees her work as a service and writing as a gift. Negotiating for better rates is both new for her and viewed by her as unseemly.[16]

To reiterate, Simran's move into television has entailed dealing with two new pressures simultaneously: having to manoeuvre a new environment with its commercial dynamics and facing familial disapproval. In the first case, the perception of invalidity stems from being a digest writer, with its own connotations of being middle- or lower middle-class and somewhat less polished in terms of lack of fluency in the English language or asserting herself. In the second instance, it stems from venturing out into a field that is seen as un-Islamic. In this context, the community of readers and writers has become the space where she feels validated. In the last few paragraphs, I have outlined some forms of support which have helped her explore the avenue of script writing. However, perhaps the more important aspect here is about unconditional affection, humility, and respect. The media industry requires the ability to market yourself and your work, and a certain competitiveness and assertion for better pay scales. In contrast, Simran takes pride in her humility and the capacity for unconditional support for co-workers. In this context, the presence of senior digest and script writers who understand and value these qualities has become Simran's cushion in the unpredictably aggressive world of media houses. In Simran's case, the comportment of respect and self-effacement, encouraged and valued in the digest community, is out of sync. It could have become an insurmountable hindrance, yet the presence of older digest writers has enabled and helped her to continue her work.

From Simran's home in Sindh, let us now proceed to Shehnaz (fictitious name), who lives in a province called Punjab. The journey to her home proved to be as interesting, if not more so, as that to Sindh, depicted in the previous chapter. Let me share it through an ethnographic note.

There were no major bus services that went directly to Shehnaz's village but there was a lesser known bus service that went to a nearby city. 'So change buses in Lahore, then in the next city, and at the third stop take the one that arrives near our village,' Shehnaz helpfully directed me. I was puzzled because she told me that seat reservations (and other plans) could be made but they were not really realistic. Ten minutes into the journey, I began to grasp what she had meant. Fifteen passengers got onto an already full bus and handed cash to the driver in return for little stools (placed in the aisle). In practical terms, this meant that a bag (or a passenger) fell on someone each time the bus turned. As we reached Lahore, I rushed over to the ticket counter and discovered that my seat reservation was not there, nor the bus that was scheduled to leave at that time. As I stood wondering what to do next, a man pointed out another bus and told me to check with the driver where it was headed. One of the stops was the city I was supposed to go to. Therefore, quite relieved, I got on. A group of women in the bus picked up some of their sleeping children and made space for me.

A few minutes after the bus started, a passenger asked the hostess for some water. 'We don't have any,' she replied and continued her conversation about food choices with the bus driver. She liked ice cream which was available in the nearby city, so we stopped. A little while later, she remembered flower garlands which another city was famous for. I began eavesdropping on the conversation, as her food and shopping preferences appeared to be a better indicator of how many and how long each of our stops was going to be. When we finally made a 'legitimate' stop, passengers got off to use the restroom. The driver seemed to remember the city I had asked him about earlier and pointed to the next bus which was parked nearby. I boarded it, thinking that I was now on the final leg.

It was night-time when I heard the name of the city to which I was going. 'Passengers going to that city should get off here.'

'Are we there?' I asked the driver.

'No.'

'But then why should I get off?' I asked, anxiously trying to read signboards in the dark.

'You see that big, colourful bus right ahead of us? You need to go on that.'

Fearing I might miss it, I stopped arguing and ran toward the next bus. An elderly, out-of-breath gentleman accompanied me in this relay race. By now, I had abandoned all hope of having a reliable schedule or timeline. A little while later, the bus stopped at a gas station, and both the driver and conductor disappeared. I told myself they had probably gone to get more passengers. However, images of armed bandits who loot buses began filtering through my mind. Just as I was about to hide my phone, Shehnaz called to ask when I would arrive. I turned to the woman next to me.

'How long till we reach that city?'

'Two, maybe three more hours.'

'Shehnaz, this lady next to me is saying three hours.'

'That can't be right; ask the bus driver.'

Finally, the bus driver appeared. 'How long till that city?'

'Two minutes.'

'Two minutes?'

'Yes, two minutes.'

I found myself laughing uncontrollably. In a strange way, comfort and certainty began to emerge from these changing timelines and unpredictable stops. The destination could be three hours away or two minutes away, but I knew I would get there eventually. I recalled my conversation with the conductor when the journey began. 'Aren't you going to give a tag for my bag?' Most bus services give you a tag against your ticket when you hand over your bags, so I felt confused.

'Baji [elder sister], you have my word; you'll get it back.' At that point I had been sceptical but throughout the journey, it was human contact and conversation that had helped navigation. Nothing on paper had been certain, but relying on others had brought me to my destination; and with my bag.

SHEHNAZ: 'INTERVIEW CHAUDHARY SAHIB TOO: YOU KNOW HOW MEN ARE'

It was late at night when I finally reached Shehnaz's home. As we settled in to sleep in the open courtyard, Shehnaz began to tell me how she had turned in one of her television scripts early so she could spend time with me. In comparison to Simran's difficulties, Shehnaz had had a relatively easy entry. Given her long, established career as a senior and popular digest writer with over 600 stories to her name, she was one of the first to be approached by a television channel. Shehnaz currently lives in a small village in Punjab which used to have limited access to television channels. Thus, when she began writing for television, she had not actually seen any of their plays.

'They said, "Do you watch our plays?" I said no. She was so surprised; she said, "If you don't watch our plays, how do you write?" and I said, "It's a gift from Allah" (*Allah ka ehsaan hai*).'

The channels approached on the basis of her position as a senior and popular digest writer. Shehnaz began writing for digests in her teens and quickly grew popular over the next few decades, gathering a loyal following of readers who related to her stories. Like most other writers, for her both script writing and digest writing are a kind of gift from God, an unpredictable process with its own dynamics.

> When I was doing my MA (Masters), I had to travel about 100 km to another city to take the final exam. On the way back, the scenery would be so nice that I wrote many stories as the sun was setting or [under] the moon [light]. Even though I had an exam the next day, I would still write about it. I would feel a commotion [*hull chull*] in me, like a tsunami … It is God-gifted, but then after my marriage,

for twelve years, I didn't write anything, and I would cry and think,
'Has God taken this away from me?'
(Muniba, have you boiled those eggs I asked you to?)

Shehnaz is a prolific television scriptwriter now, and given the
popularity of her plays, one of the highest paid television soap
writers. However, as I sat with her on her bed that morning, her
most conspicuous role was that of a busy homemaker. Milk had to
be boiled, breakfast had to be served to a fussy family, and there was
a large family of in-laws who dropped in unexpectedly and stayed
on indefinitely. All this was interspersed through our conversation.
Chaudhary sahib, her husband, sat in the other room but Shehnaz
called him in, whispering to me, 'Interview him too—you know
what men are like'. I kept the tape recorder on and began to ask him
quickly conjured questions about his life and ancestry. The next
morning, as we sat together in the living room, Shehnaz's mother-
in-law joined us. I began to prepare myself to ask her questions and
record them so that she would also feel included but stopped when
I heard Shehnaz introduce me as a friend. She told her mother-
in-law that I had invited her to Islamabad but, as Shehnaz could
not travel, I had come to the village to meet her. There was no
mention of her work as a writer. After she left, Shehnaz began
to share the lack of validation she feels from her in-laws. 'You've
seen my mother-in-law: for her, I'm nothing. Writing, television,
all this means nothing to her, but if I had status or an important
post [ohda], then she would have thought of me as something.' At
first, women were not allowed to watch TV at her in-laws'. This has
changed now, and most of the daughters-in-law have a television
set in their bedrooms. However, Shehnaz's mother-in-law does not
watch TV, nor has she ever read any of Shehnaz's stories.

As a successful script writer, Shehnaz earns well and contributes
to the household for buying land and paying her son's tuition fees.
Because her income is from television script writing, it doesn't
have the same status; however, it has enabled her to fulfil her own

material needs more comfortably. She shared that her husband sometimes hands over thousands of rupees at a time (from the seasonal agricultural income on his land) but she never feels comfortable spending it on herself. 'I think, what if he asks for the balance [*hisaab maang lain*]? But with my own income, I can say, get me a new pair of shoes, or get me new clothes. He gets me these things too but with my own income, it's different.'

In this context, script writing provides her a reliable source of money earned from home. Shehnaz has never visited a channel office or a production house. Contracts and scripts are mailed, and one-liners are discussed during phone conversations. Thus, her domestic life and its rhythms remain uninterrupted. Domestic responsibilities take over the day, so it is only after 10 pm that she can work on her scripts. Previously, this time was reserved for digest writing, and in a sense she could enter her inner world. Now, given the time pressures of work for television, this time is frequently devoted to other deadlines.

> You see, scripts are just commercial; there are no inner feelings. In a digest story [*afsana*], you have inner feelings. I'll tell you honestly, I never feel anything when I'm writing a script ... It's a simple thing to understand [*seedhi si baat hai*]; we don't write a script that deeply.

To some degree this is because of the rigid frameworks to which they must adhere. For instance, Shehnaz usually based her digest stories in a rural setting but for her scripts, she has to adopt an urban setting. This is partly because of the production costs involved in taking the crew to a rural location and partly because channels perceive that their audiences prefer urban settings.

Like other television script writers, Shehnaz has continued to write for digests even although this does not provide any real monetary compensation. Her latest story is about a boy from the rural areas and a girl who lives in the city. Shehnaz framed her story as humorous but at a different level it reflects certain dynamics of her own life and the search for respect.

> The story is kind of comical. When the father of the girl asks the boy how much he has studied, the boy's grandmother replies instead. She says he failed his tenth-grade exam, but he has so many buffaloes. Vehicles from the Golden Milk Company drop in all day long. Then the father says, 'Is my daughter going to take baths in all this milk?' Later, the boy shares that he's actually educated and has a PhD in dairy farming. He says to them, 'You're so shallow. You only judged me on my clothes and appearance; you didn't see my deeper self.'

Shehnaz is highly educated and holds two masters degrees. Her plays are extremely popular, and she gets paid well by the television channels. However, her voice is not really heard. The authenticity and space to negotiate or validate her own ideas about the kinds of plays that need to be written are absent. In this context, like the boy in the story who was judged on the basis of his appearance alone, like other digest writers, she too is judged on appearances of class and gender. Mispronouncing certain English words or not using English at all, lacking the mobility which is often taken for granted by other women, are all factors that add to a certain kind of persona; an image that lends itself to class dynamics and the politics that accompanies it. Simultaneously, at home she is not really seen as a writer. Script writing is a source of income, but one that is not really granted the status or significance an earning family member would otherwise receive. In this context, the digest world becomes a niche and a resting place. In Simran's case, the digest community often cushions her from the challenges of negotiating and working for television, whereas for Shehnaz, it appears to be a space where she can be herself. As we settled in to sleep in her open courtyard, I saw her checking the text messages sent by readers and writers during the day.

'"Tip for losing weight: drink coconut water"—where do they think I live, Malaysia? Oh, there are three missed calls from Shabana.' As she replied to the messages and called back, I see her face change. The tired and tense image of the homemaker disappeared, giving way to a youthful, lively woman. The same liveliness that had been there in our interactions over the phone began shining through again.

To reiterate, this chapter tells the story of digest writers' search of respect and validity by examining how they make sense of their entry into television and the challenges they have to face, in particular with regard to the social perception of not being 'real' writers. I suggest that although their plays do pander to certain commercial or base desires, these television depictions of digest fiction also act as an avenue for what can best be described as little slivers of reality: personal experiences of middle-class women which they rescue from oblivion. I have presented key themes to show that the struggle for respect is not just in the public realm but also the private one of family. Finally, I narrowed the ethnographic gaze to two writers to show the specific forms the struggle for respect takes in their lives.

NOTES

1. Given the mainstream popularity of the play, the writer's name is common knowledge, and therefore it has not been changed here.
2. 'Voh humsafar tha magar uss se humnavai na thi/ke dhoop chaon ka alam raha judai na thi.'
3. The drama serial closely follows the digest novel, and both open with a simply dressed Khirad (played by Mahira Khan) entering an upscale office building with files in her hand. In the next scene, she tells Ashar (played by Fawad Khan) that she had a daughter from him who urgently needs heart surgery and has the DNA reports to prove he is the father. Ashar's mother (played by Atiqa Odho) and her niece, Sarah (played by Naveen Khan), are both against this marriage, the mother because she feels her son has married below his social status, and Sara because she is in love with Ashar. They

create misunderstandings between the couple, who stay separated for a few
years but eventually reunite.

4. 'Understanding the Humsafar hype', *Newsline*, 2012.

5. Of course, the digest writers themselves were an audience. They were aware
   that it would be submitted as a dissertation, and later perhaps circulated as a
   book. However, the potential orbits of circulation were largely disconnected
   from their own. They also knew their perspectives had been woven through
   different theories, but the actual paper was of little interest to them. It was
   work that would allow me to complete my PhD, write a book, and record
   some of what they had said; they supported me in that but were less invested
   in what was in the actual work, perhaps because the language was not their
   own.

6. He begins his argument with Marcel Proust's insightful conclusion of his
   magnum opus, 'True life, life finally discovered and illuminated, the only
   life therefore really lived, is literature; that life which, in a sense, at every
   moment inhabits all men as well as the artist' (1954: 895, quoted in Fassin,
   2014: 40).

7. Fassin (2014) suggests that although good fiction presents profound
   truths about life which we as anthropologists can only hope to express,
   nevertheless, our ethnographic work carries the stamp of validity. Our works
   may be presented before smaller audiences, but the status of ethnography
   as 'real' endows empirical validity. In other words, the same license of
   imagination which allows artists to mould their raw material deprives it of
   some of its authenticity.

8. This is a common practice. Digest-turned-script writers often develop one-
   liners which are handed over to junior digest writers. The script is written
   by them but supervised by the former. A practise not very different from a
   co-authored paper, and it enables new writers to enter the field by lending
   them the credibility of senior writers.

9. The only other play that has depicted an aspect of the digest world is *Bewafai
   Tumharay Naam* (Betrayal for You; 2015). Rather than a writer, one of the
   principal characters is the editor of a digest. However, it was written by
   Faseeh Bari Khan, who is not himself a digest writer.

10. As Fareeda steps out of the world of her stories, the audience is introduced
    to the reality of the restricted finances and anxious parents that texture her
    everyday life.

11. She sends her stories under the pseudonym of Rashk-i Hina (Pride of
    Henna). Making sure that no one can overhear her, she calls the editor to
    ask about her stories. The editor, Binte Hawa (Daughter of Eve), tells Fareeda
    the stories have not been read yet and puts down the phone, muttering about
    the kind of people with whom she has to deal.

12. *Bahishti Zewar* is a volume of Islamic beliefs and practices written by Maulana Ashraf Ali Thanvi. It is a handbook of jurisprudence especially for the education of girls and women.

13. Khalida Ahmed, '*Dil-e-Shikastha ke hazar dagh* (A thousand marks on the fragile heart)' *Pakeeza*, March 1985.

14. The Sindhi fiction writer Noorul Huda Shah has also written a popular book entitled *The Secrets of Haveli*.

15. Similar to a social security number, this proof of identity is necessary for any formal contract or transaction.

16. Given that her current work is headed by Raheela, the rates were negotiated by the latter, and Simran did not have to deal directly with the production house. However, before this project, she did need to negotiate and was guided by the long-distance network of other digest writers. Simran initially sent her script to both a production house and a channel.

Conclusion

As I write these lines, there are several pages scattered around me with outlines for the concluding section of this work. Some are in column form with points under main themes, others in bright colours with half-image, half-word depictions. One of the pages also carries a half-completed digest story. Over the past few months, I have pushed aside writing the story as a treat to be savoured once I am done completing the work on this book. However, the more I think about it, the more it seems that these are not airtight compartments: story writing and ethnographic writing require the same set of skills.

THE STORY OF THIS BOOK

The guidance given by digest writers appears as true for ethnography as it does for a story. 'You have to portray the space where you want to take your readers.' The point is to show the way the air feels, point out the colours, the sounds, and smells of that particular spatial context. As I elaborate in 'Chapter 2', there is no real spatiality in the digest community. I could describe digest offices, libraries, book stalls, or the homes visited or lived in. However, the real dwellings of readers and writers are their stories. These stories are not just fictional digest stories but also those which they relate to one another about their lives. Absence and anonymity lead to a norm of engagement where identities are formed through conversations rather than the other way around.

In our usual everyday interactions, our identities contour our conversations and what we share with others. The texture of our conversation or the paths they can take are paved by our identity

200

or role in that context. In the digest community, rather than the usual introductory identity markers of class, ethnicity, age, and/or disciplinary background, women approach one another on the basis of fictional stories. Given the interweaving of desires, sentiments, morality, and lived experiences which suffuse each writer's story, these become doorways to their inner emotional landscapes. Readers and writers get to know and place one another by the stories they endorse. These in turn lead to conversations over the phone and depictions of their personal lives. The dynamics of absence and anonymity allow them to tell whatever story they wish. This is not in terms of lies or deception, as such, but through a different form of telling.

As the philosopher Todd May (2015) suggests, we usually understand ourselves through the stories we choose to tell about our lives. These stories correspond to real events but have to be woven into a narrative form through certain themes (such as alienation, struggle, strength, or connection). Each incident has a million vantage points, and the vantage point we choose to frame it through often reflects our inner world more than it does the outer, 'objective' reality. Alternatively, as the saying goes, interpretations tell more about the interpreter than they do about the subject. In our usual everyday interactions, our identities get in the way. What we choose to share of our feelings about incidents or relationships is often shaped by the identity we hold in that context. To give a simple example, the way you would share news of a parent's death with a distant colleague is different from how you would do so with a sibling. The incident is the same but the feelings that will be shared in one context are very different from those which can be shared in another. There is also the factor of shared reality. For instance, we cannot really depict a family member as loving and warm if others have witnessed our interactions with him/her and know otherwise. Physical proximity leads to a shared reality, which in certain ways hinders our capacity to tell a different story (as the digest story about the two friends shared in 'Chapter 2' aptly demonstrates). In the digest community, a person is free to tell the story she wants to, both about her life as well as the world around her. There are no roles to live up to and therefore feelings and emotions suffuse the conversation. As I point out in 'Chapter 1', I would often find myself sharing details of my life (and emotions about them) with digest writers which I would not usually share with others. In this context, this becomes a space where a person tells the stories she wants, and this particular emergence of feelings and new ways of relating the same incidents is a specific characteristic of this community.

The fictional stories are not as such really fictional. They are often drawn from real life, a person's own or another's, and depict felt emotions and engagements with contemporary realities of living as a woman in Pakistan. Even those that pander to frivolous desires for wealth or romance are often an inverted image of emotional or material deprivations. Lived realities of financial constraints and neglectful husbands are turned (inverted) into imagined stories about nurturing men who drive expensive cars and bring flowers each day.

These emotional worlds are shared and thrive through contact with another reader or writer. The stories or conversations shape the friendship but in sharing an emotional world (through depictions of lived or desired relationships), a person also forms a bond with the listener. A person is known through her emotional landscape or inner world. However, it is in telling and sharing that the inner world (of lived impossibilities or desired possibilities) becomes visible to the person concerned. In other words, a person dwells in the inner world through these conversations. Thus, these conversations are as much of a dwelling as the fictional stories.

Women engage with this genre through digest stories; therefore, this book also examines fictional narratives from this genre. This is not in the context of literary analysis but to show what these dwellings look and feel like, how they are created and inhabited in various ways by different writers and readers.

Let us now move from *manzar nigari* (scene setting) to the 'logic' of this story. Stories can be written on the basis of *manzar nigari* and *laffazi* (wordiness) but this can lead to a sense of confusion for the reader. The writers who were guiding me in writing the digest story emphasised that sentences which define the story need to be amplified (*unn ki baazghasht aaye*) so that the logic of the story becomes clear. Although digest writers call it logic, I understand this to be the spirit of the story. This refers to the main theme, the axle around which the story revolves or the anchor that holds it. Discerning this spirit or logic is a considerable challenge. Ideally, this is clear before you start writing so that the *khayal* (thought or idea) is visible but mostly it is not apparent when you begin the process of writing. It is often towards the end that you realise what you actually wanted to say. Some points are within the creation (*takhleeq ke andar hota hai),* and eventually, it is the creation itself that tells you what that is.

The spirit/logic of this book appears to have changed form at different stages. The first academic writing was a response. The idea was to bring forth voices of dissent in this genre which raised important questions with regard to issues such as domestic violence and financial independence. The second work was not a response as such but a 'look what I found'. The initial fieldwork experience had led to interaction with this community. The focus of that work was how these bonds are formed over mobile phones without visual cues. Based on fieldwork notes that contained interviews with writers, that work was more difficult than the first. Reading the notes felt like working on a jigsaw puzzle where the picture changed each time I began to assemble the pieces and search for a form. Finally, giving up the search for key themes, I began writing as thoughts occurred to me. One afternoon, as I walked toward the kitchen, I recalled a sentence. During the interviews some of the writers had asked, 'But you haven't told me about yourself?' with overtones of invitation and confusion. The curiosity at this question replaced the anxiety of 'doing it right' and led to anthropological work on this community as a space where women engaged with one another on the basis of the shared reality of being a woman in Pakistan. This path in turn led to the three key themes explored here: attachment, articulation, and agency. The primary question was: How do women engage with this genre and one another as digest writers and readers, notwithstanding differences of ethnicity, age, and class.

THE NEXT STEP

To explore what the next step of this trajectory might be, let me briefly share some loose ends, paths that were explored during fieldwork but relegated to later examination. One key avenue is the circulation of this genre in wider arenas. The engagement with electronic media has led to several interesting developments. Strata that do not usually read digests, such as the unschooled and the English-speaking elite, are now engaging with digest stories in its televised form.

An intriguing example of intertextual engagement with the digest genre is a popular TV serial, *Quddusi Saheb ki Beva* (Mr Quddusi's widow). It revolves around the everyday domestic life of a middle-class woman and her adult children. However, middle-class norms of respectability are overturned because her only son enjoys cross-dressing and dancing like a woman, one daughter is involved with several married men, while the other is romantically involved with her driver. This could be seen as carnivalesque comedy, but its dialogues often refer to digest writers and their serials, showing an intertextual engagement with the genre. More specifically, its writer, Faseeh Bari Khan, in his interview with me, highlighted responding to stereotypical notions of womanhood by digest writers as a primary motivation behind his play. As digest writers' vantage points of women's lived experiences in Pakistan circulate through highly popular dramas, there is also an emergent counter-narrative that transforms the gendered norms usually espoused by digest stories. Let me explain this overturning through an ethnographic note about visiting the shoot of *QSKB*.

As I walked toward the house where the drama serial *Quddusi Saheb ki Beva* was being filmed, I felt my sense of exhaustion morphing into excitement. This popular TV serial revolves around the everyday domestic life of a middle-class woman and her adult children. A common theme is the blurring of gendered subject positions. This blurring is most evident in her tall, manly son who enjoys cross-dressing and dancing like a woman. This includes holding his forefinger between his teeth, cocking his head, or coyly smiling with downcast eyes. These are gestures that are commonly known as *ada'ain*—a word that has connotations of women's flirtatious display, in contrast to male flirting, which is usually referred to as *taarrhna* (staring) or line *maarna* (attempting to elicit a response).

A man opened the gate and told me that no filming was in progress. However, when I said that the director and writer gave me this address, he let me in and took me to the upper floor. Various young men, cameras, audio mics, and lights flooded the space and two young actors stood in a corner arguing about the script. A little while later, I saw the actor who plays the role of the son, Wudood Ahmed. The actor, Waqar Hussain, runs a salon and does make-up for commercial shoots. He explained that he saw his character, Wudood, as 'an innocent, pure spirit' (*maasoom paak rooh*) who has only seen women around him and was therefore unaware of what it is like to be masculine. He seemed silent when I mentioned how Khawaja siras enjoy seeing the play but opened up when I spoke about my own regular engagement with the serial. He asked me if other people in the US also watched it and appeared pleased when I told him that some of them do. The director had introduced me as visiting scholar from the US, so my academic interest in the play appeared to be a way of brokering first-world prestige on a third-world phenomenon.

In the scene being filmed, Hina Dilpazeer was playing Illaichi (cardamom), the khawaja sira. Her clothes were feminine but the makeup was loud, with dark powder on her chin and cheeks to indicate stubble. Filming was a painfully slow process made more difficult by the heat because the fans were turned off to avoid sound intrusion. I felt perspiration trickling down my back and was amazed at the actors' stamina as they performed under bright lights. In this scene, Illachi was visiting a family into which Wudood was supposed to marry. The director sat at the table with the script in his hand and repeated each line before the cameras rolled. The two cameramen began smiling when Illaichi said, 'So I saw this rickshaw driver; his face was pleasant to look at, so I jumped in' (*aik buzka rickshay walay ki shakal achi thi toh andar jaa ke baith gai*). Each line was repeated twice, first in a group setting and then with a close-up of the actor's face while the rest of the group rested. The director explained that this was done to keep the audience engaged through different angles, called long shot and close shot. The five-minute scene took over two hours. There were several breaks: A young girl complained (to no one in particular) that the burger she had asked for had not arrived; there was some discussion on what the word *tarawa* used in the script could be (the director did not know but Dilpazeer explained that it is the term khawaja siras use for makeup); a girl asked if she should have her head covered for the scene. A little while later, two men walked in and began watching the performance; the actors complained, and the men were asked to leave. Just as they walked out, the call for prayers began at the local mosque, and recording had to be stopped again because it interfered with the audio recording.

There is a frequent blurring of gendered binaries not just through Wudood's character but also the various roles that the actor Hina Dilpazeer plays. When the serial began in 2012, she was playing four different roles. As the serial progressed, more characters were introduced, and her roles grew to 22. Her roles also began to cross gender lines as two new characters (a khawaja sirah and a male servant) were introduced in 2013. Subsequent to the popularity of this theme, another play entitled *Bubbly Darling* (2015) by the same writer, Faseeh Bari Khan, has the same motif.

Bubbly Darling (aired as an Eid special) revolves around two families. The first comprises two sisters and their younger brother. Women actors play the sisters but gender boundaries are overturned through their intimidating personalities and reputation for violence. The two sisters earn a livelihood for the family by renting furniture to people, and several scenes revolve around them beating up men who delay paying their rent. The second family is a nuclear one of a young woman and her parents. Hina Dilpazeer plays the role of her dominant father while Waqar (the same actor who played Wudood Ahmed in *QSKB*) plays the role of her mother.

Men have played women's roles in both ancient theatre and modern-day television.[1] However, a woman playing a man, as Dilpazeer does in *QSKB* and *Bubbly Darling*, is a rare and new occurrence in Pakistan's electronic media that has occurred in conjunction with the proliferation of the use of stories by digest writers in the electronic media. The relative impermeability of this boundary (from female to male) in the media echoes its relative impermeability in Pakistan's cultural field. Blackwood (1986, 1991) suggests that in gender-stratified or patriarchal societies, women are not allowed to take on masculine roles because it is seen as a threat to men's privilege. This is valid but cannot be generalised as there are several gender-stratified societies where there is a casual acceptance of female born individuals assuming a male persona.[2]

At a different level, this is also reflective of subtle shifts in conventional understandings of gender in Pakistan. Till recently, there has been an absence of role reversal from woman to man in both media and society. There have always been same-sex relationships between women but a woman crossing gender boundaries to become a man or assume a masculine identity (by changing her name) continues to be rare. The peculiar dynamics of social perceptions became evident in 2007 in a case filed in the

Lahore High Court. A woman named Shahzina was being forced to marry against her will. She appealed to the court on the basis that she was already legally married to and living with her cousin Shumail. Her family countered that the marriage was void because Shumail was not a man. This led to a media frenzy. The liberal press defended them as two women who had chosen not men but each other, whereas the more right-wing press condemned it. Both assumed that it was a same-sex marriage. However, Shumail, who had undergone two sex-change operations, saw himself as a man.[3] To determine the case, the court ordered a medical examination, and based on the results, concluded that the lack of male genitalia meant Shumail was lying about being male. He was sentenced to jail, and the determination of location—women's jail rather than men's—further reinforced this conception.[4] A year later there was a case of a woman wishing to undergo a sex-change operation. The same court, under a different judge and a different government, proclaimed that there was no restriction on such operations and she could 'become' a man. The following year, 2009, the Supreme Court introduced the category of third gender in national identity cards.

I would argue that the question of what it means to live as a woman in contemporary Pakistan is a central one in digest fiction. Given the variety of backgrounds of readers and writers, there are numerous and diverse answers to this question. However, simultaneously there is a certain contextualisation that occurs partly on the basis of editorial control and partly because of the perceived sensibilities of digest readers. However, over the past decade, as fiction by digest writers circulates in new spheres, there are new questions being raised about how it is contextualised (asked and answered in digest stories). *QSKB* and *Bubbly Darling* then become one particular form of contestation.

In conclusion, each academic engagement (particularly with long-term projects, such as a book or dissertation) is also a personal exploration. The time and energy they require of us cannot be given without an emotional investment in the question being examined. Each of our works is a different path that reconsiders the same underlying question. As I read the previous sections which chart my trajectory toward this work and where it might go next, the underlying question appears to be that of bridging otherness. I think of my own split identities (identifying with two ethnicities; having grown up in Pakistan, part of the Global South, but with higher education in the Global North), and the emotional investment in attempting to bridge two different worlds becomes apparent.

Finally, how we can look at others (and ourselves) and see what we did not hitherto see is a central question in every anthropological exploration. Perhaps the beckoning of this question is also about connections and flows of which we are intuitively aware. There are no neat dichotomies of self/ other, world/ human, reality/ imagination. Our relationship with ourselves influences our relationship with others. For instance, certainty in our own worth leads us to also gauge worth in others. The same goes for doubt and mistrust. Similarly, the world is outside of us but we filter and shape it through our perceptions. In this context, as anthropologists our work is perhaps as much about the gravitational pull of these flows that overturn dichotomies as it is about bridging otherness in the outer world.

NOTES

1. For instance, the host of a Pakistani talk show, Begum Nawazish Ali, was a man who dressed up as an upper-class woman and interviewed politicians and media celebrities.
2. See Sharyn Davies, *Gender Diversity in Indonesia: Sexuality, Islam and Queer Selves*, Routledge, 2011.
3. These entailed the removal of breasts and uterus and indicate that she was not born intersexed but female.
4. Ironically, the lack of male genitalia in some sense also saved the couple from Section 377. This clause identifies severe punishment for 'indecent or

unnatural conduct'. However, the act of penetration, needed for this law to be applied, was missing in this case. The last media reports (at the time of this writing) indicate that the two were eventually released on bail and are awaiting a retrial.

Bibliography

Abu Lughod, L. (2005). *Dramas of Nationhood: The Politics of Television in Egypt.* Chicago, IL: University of Chicago Press.

———. (1991). Writing Against Culture. In Richard G. Fox ed., *Recapturing Anthropology: Working in the Present.* Santa Fe: School of American Research Press.

———. (2002). Do Muslim Women Really Need Saving? Anthropological Reflections on Cultural Relativism and Its Others. *American Anthropologist* 104 (3): 783–90.

———. (1986). *Veiled Sentiments: Honor and Poetry in a Bedouin Society.* California: University of California Press.

Ahmed, K. (2004). Urban Women Rebels: Voices of Dissent in Urdu Popular Fiction. In *Sustainable Development: Bridging the Research/ Policy Gaps in Southern Contexts: Social Policy.* Oxford: Oxford University Press.

Ali, K. A. (2005). Courtesans in the Living Room. *Annual of Urdu Studies,* Vol. 20: 274–9.

———. (2011). Progressives and 'Perverts': Partition Stories and Pakistan's Future. *Social Text,* Vol. 29 (3) 108: 1–29.

———. (2012). Women, Work and Public Spaces: Conflict and Coexistence in Karachi's Poor Neighborhoods. *International Journal of Urban and Regional Research* 36 (3): 585–605.

———. (2006). Strength of the State meets the Strength of the Street: The 1972 Labour Struggle in Karachi. In Naveeda Khan ed., *Beyond Crisis: Re-Evaluating Pakistan* (Critical Asian Studies). London/New York: Routledge.

———. (2004). Pulp Fictions: Reading Pakistani Domesticity, *Social Text,* Vol. 22 (1): 123–45.

Anderson, B. (1991). *Imagined Communities. Reflections on the Origin and Spread of Nationalism.* London: Verso Books.

Appadurai, Arjun (1991). Global Ethnoscapes: Notes and Queries for a Transnational Anthropology. In Richard Fox ed., *Recapturing Anthropology*. Santa Fe: School of American Research Press.

Bari, F. and Khattak S. (2001). Power Configurations in Public and Private Arenas: The Women's Movement's Response. In Anita Weiss and Zulfiqar Gillani eds., *Power and Civil Society in Pakistan*. Karachi: SDPI/Oxford University Press.

Bendix, R. (1997). *In Search of Authenticity: The Formation of Folklore Studies*. Madison: University of Wisconsin Press.

Berlant, Lauren (2008). *The Female Complaint: The Unfinished Business of Sentimentality in American Culture*. Durham: Duke University Press Books.

Blackwood, E. (2005). Tombois in West Sumatra: Constructing Masculinity and Erotic Desire. In Ellen Lewin ed., *Feminist Anthropology: A Reader*. Oxford: Blackwell.

Bordo, S. (1993). The Body and the Reproduction of Femininity. In Susan Bordo ed., *Unbearable Weight: Feminism, Western Culture, and the Body*. Berkeley: University of California Press.

Bourdieu, Pierre (1990). Opinion Polls: A Science Without a Scientist. In Mathew Adamson trans., *In Other Words: Essays toward a Reflexive Sociology*. Stanford: Stanford University Press.

——. (1977). *Outline of a Theory of Practice: Objective Limits of Objectivism*. Cambridge: Cambridge University Press.

Breen, M. and Blumenfeld W. (2005). *Butler Matters: Judith Butler's Impact on Feminist and Queer Studies*. Aldershot, Burlington: Ashgate.

Butler, J. (2005). *Giving an Account of Oneself*. New York: Fordham University Press.

——. (2006). *Gender Trouble: Feminism and the Subversion of Identity*. New York: Routledge.

——. (1993). *Bodies that Matter: On The Discursive Limits of 'Sex'*. New York: Routledge.

——. (2009). *Undoing Gender*. New York: Routledge.

——. and Salih, S. (2003). Interview with Butler. In *The Judith Butler Reader*. Malden, MA: Blackwell Publications.

Csordas, T. (1993). Somatic Modes of Attention. *Cultural Anthropology*, Vol. 8 (2): 135–56.

Cvetskovich, A. 1992. *Mixed Feelings: Feminism, Mass Culture, and Victorian Sensationalism*. New Brunswick: Rutgers University Press.

Davies, S. (2010). *Gender Diversity in Indonesia: Sexuality, Islam and Queer Selves*. New York: Routledge.

Deleuze, G. (1987). *A Thousand Plateaus*. tr. Brian Massumi. Minneapolis: University of Minnesota Press.

Derrida, J. (1967). *Of Grammatology*. Baltimore: Johns Hopkins University Press.

Djebar, A. and Blair, D. (1993). *Fantasia, an Algerian Cavalcade*. Portsmouth: Heinemann.

Doty, M. (2010). *The Art of Description: World into Word*. Minneapolis: Graywolf Press.

Fassin, D. (2014). True life, real lives: Revisiting the boundaries between ethnography and fiction. *American Anthologist*, 41 (1): 40–55.

Fortun, K. (2012). Ethnography in Late Industrialism. *Cultural Anthropology*, 27 (3): 446–64.

Foucault, M. (1978). *Discipline and Punish*. Trans. Alan Sheridan. New York: Random House.

———. (1970). *Order of Things: An Archeology of the Human Sciences*. New York: Random House.

———. (1984). What is an Author?. In Paul Rainbow ed., *The Foucault Reader*. New York: Pantheon Books.

———, and Hurley, R. (1990). *The History of Sexuality: An Introduction*. New York: Vintage Books.

Ganti, T. (2009). The Limits of Decency and the Decency of Limits. In Raminder Kaur and William Mazzarella, *Censorship in South Asia: Cultural Regulation from Sedition to Seduction*. Indiana: Indiana University Press.

Gaudio, R. (2009). *Allah Made Us: Sexual Outlaws in an Islamic African City*. New Directions in Ethnography. Oxford: Wiley-Blackwell.

Gregg, M., and Seigworth G. (2010). *The Affect Theory Reader*. Durham: Duke University Press.

Grosz, E. (1986). Philosophy, Subjectivity and the Body. In C. Pateman and E. Gross eds., *Feminist Challenges. Social and Political Theory*. C. Pateman. Boston: Northeastern University Press, 125–44.

———. (1994). *Volatile Bodies: Toward a Corporeal Feminism*. Bloomington: Indiana University Press.

————. (1995). *Space, Time and Perversion: Essays on the Politics of Bodies.* New York: Routledge.

Ginsburg, F., Abu Lughod, L., and Larkin B. (2002). Introduction. In *Media Worlds: Anthropology on New Terrain.* Berkley: University of California Press.

Hapgood, L. (2010). *Margins of Desire: The Suburbs in Fiction and Culture 1880–1925.* Manchester/New York: Manchester University Press.

Harlow, B. (1992). *Barred: Women, Writing, and Political Detention.* Hanover: Wesleyan University Press.

Hartigan, J. (2010). *What Can You Say? America's National Conversation on Race.* Stanford: Stanford University Press.

Heidegger, M. (1971). Language. In *Poetry, Language, Thought,* trans. Albert Hofstadter. New York: Harper & Row.

Humphrey, C. (2005). Ideology in Infrastructure. Architecture and Soviet Imagination. *Journal of the Royal Anthropological Institute* 11(1): 39–58.

Jacob, W. (2011). *Working out Egypt: Effendi Masculinity and Subject Formation in Colonial Modernity, 1870–1940.* Durham: Duke University Press.

Jensen, M. (1980). Women and Romantic Fiction: A Study of Harlequin Enterprises, Romances and Readers. PhD dissertation, Macmaster University.

Kaur, R. and Mazzarella, W. (2009). Between Sedition and Seduction: Thinking Censorship in South Asia. In *Censorship in South Asia: Cultural Regulation from Sedition to Seduction.* Indiana: Indiana University Press.

Khattak, S. (2001). Women, Work and Empowerment. In S. Khattak and A. Sayeed eds., *Women's Work and Empowerment Issues in an Era of Economic Liberalisation: A Case Study of Pakistan's Urban Manufacturing Sector.* Pilar.

Kittler, F. (2006). Lightening and Series-Event and Thunder. *Theory Culture Society* 23:63. DOI: 10.1177/0263276406069883.

Larkin, B. (2004). Degraded Images, Distorted Sounds: Nigerian Video and the Infrastructure of Piracy. *Public Culture* 16, no. 2: 289–314.

————. (2008). *Signal and Noise: Media, Infrastructure, and Urban Culture in Nigeria.* Durham: Duke University Press.

Littau, K. (2006). *Theories of Reading: Books, Bodies, and Bibliomania.* Cambridge: Malden; MA: Polity.

Mahmood, S. (2012). *Politics of Piety: The Islamic Revival and the Feminist Subject.* Princeton: Princeton University Press.

Marcus, S. (2007). *Between Women: Friendship, Desire and Marriage in Victorian England.* Princeton: Princeton University Press.

Mauss, M. (1967). *The Gift: Forms and Functions of Exchange in Archaic Societies,* trans. Ian Cunnison, with an introduction by E. E. Evans-Pritchard. New York: Norton.

May, T. (2005). *Gilles Deleuze: An Introduction.* New York: Cambridge University Press.

———. (2015). *A Significant Life: Human Meaning in a Silent Universe.* Chicago: University of Chicago Press.

Minault, G. (1998). *Secluded Scholars: Women's Education and Muslim Social Reform in Colonial India* (Gender Studies). Delhi/New York: Oxford University Press.

Mittermaier, A. (2010). *Dreams that Matter: Egyptian Landscapes of the Imagination.* Los Angeles: University of California Press.

Mohanty, C. (1991). Cartographies of Struggle: Third World Women and the Politics of Feminism. In Chandra Mohanty Talpade, Anne Russo, and Lourdes Torres eds., *Third World Women and the Politics of Feminism.* Bloomington: Indiana University Press.

Pervez, S. (1988). Analysis of Mass Media Appealing to Women. National Institute of Psychology, Islamabad, Pakistan. Monograph no. 8.

Radway, J. (1984). *Reading the Romance: Women, Patriarchy and Popular Literature.* Chapel Hill: University of North Carolina Press.

Rajagopal, A. (2001). *Politics after Television: Hindu Nationalism and the Reshaping of the Public in India.* Cambridge: Cambridge University Press.

Ring, Laura A. (2006). *Zenana: Everyday Peace in a Karachi Apartment Building.* Bloomington: Indiana University Press.

Sacks, O. (2010). *The Mind's Eye.* New York: Random House.

Said, E. (1983, 2003). *The World, The Text and the Critic.* New York: Harvard University Press.

Skalli, L. (2008). *Through a Local Prism: Gender, Globalization, and Identity in Moroccan Women's Magazines.* Lanham: Lexington Books.

Spivak, G. (1984): Can the Subaltern Speak?. In Patrick Williams and Laura Chrisman eds., *Colonial Discourse and Post Colonial Theory*, ed. (New York: Columbia University Press.

Stewart, K. (2011). Atmospheric Attunements. *Society and Space* 20: 445–53.

———. (2007). *Ordinary Affects*. Durham: Duke University Press.

———. (2013): Regionality. *Geographical Review* 103 (2): 275–84.

Talwar, V. (1989). Feminist Consciousness in Women's Journals in Hindi: 1910–1920. In K Sangari and S. Vaid eds., *Recasting Women: Essays in Colonial History*. New Delhi: Kali for Women, 204–32.

Tharu, S., and Lalitha, K. (eds.) (1991). *Women Writing in India: 600 B.C. to the Present*. New York: Feminist Press at the City University of New York.

Wittgenstein, L. (1953). *Philosophical Investigations* tr. G. E. M. Anscombe. New York: Macmillan.

Wekker, G. (1999). What's Identity Got to do with It?: Rethinking Identity in Light of the Mati Work in Suriname. In Evelyn Blackwood and Saskia E. Wieringa, *Female Desires, Same Sex and Transgender Practices across Cultures*. New York: Columbia University Press.

Zavella, P. (1993). Feminist Insider Dilemmas: Constructing Ethnic Identity with 'Chicana' Informants. In Louise Lamphere, Helena Ragone, Patricia Zavella eds., *Situated Lives: Gender and Culture in Everyday Life*. (2014). Routledge.

Index

217